D.E.B.T.

The Relationship Edition:

HOW TO STOP LETTING MONEY GET IN THE WAY OF LOVE

D.E.B.T.

The Relationship Edition:

HOW TO STOP LETTING MONEY GET IN THE WAY OF LOVE

BY JOSEPH LORICK

Printed in the United States of America

First Printing, 2015

ISBN-13: 978-0692382509

(Agape Christian Books Gifts & Music)

ISBN-10: 069238250X

All Inquiries can be sent to:

Agape Christian Books Gifts & Music

5209 York Rd

Baltimore, MD 21212

www.moneyetiquette.com

joseph.lorick@moneyetiquette.com

Sara Mason: copyeditor

Tracey Brown: cover photographer

Rachelle Lorick: cover photo make-up artist

Thank you, Mrs. Lorick

A little more than six years ago, you and I stepped in front of our minister and agreed to share the rest of our lives together. We began our marriage full of personal ideas about what marriage should be and the roles of husband and wife. I thought a wife should be ready to put all her trust in God and her husband the moment she said, "I do". You believed that your life as an individual was over because my priorities would trump your own. We both believed our background as Christians and both of us coming from two parent households prepared us for everything we would encounter as a married couple. It turns out we both were wrong, and needed a lot of time to grow. After only a few months of being married, our relationship began to reach new lows. You felt distant from me because I couldn't overcome my disappointment in not having a wife that met all my premarital expectations, and you struggled with the same problem. We were supposed to be the couple that didn't have these problems and extended the honeymoon phase for years. Talk about being delusional. Six months into our marriage we were both wondering if it would last. All of our problems were tied to unrealistic expectations and a lack of understanding, but oncoming financial problems only made things worse.

We were in the midst of the worst economic recession the United States had ever experienced; save the great depression. One year prior to us getting married, I purchased my first home and was making enough money to pay all my bills and put some money into savings accounts. I was sure I'd prepared myself to take on the costs of marriage and fulfill my duties as a provider. You only had a car note, a small furniture loan, and little student loan debt, so I believed that I could pay your bills along with my bills. I only wanted you to focus on growing in your career and being a Godly wife, but those expectations didn't reflect reality. While I was busy planning for a perfect future, the economy was preparing to ruin those plans. Just one year into our marriage this disaster hit us hard. The stock market began to tank, the mortgage crisis showed its ugly face, banks were failing, the federal government began bailing out private businesses, and I just so happened to be working for one of the biggest banks in the world. In response to this economic crisis, my employer made some changes to our pay structure. I was no longer bringing in the money I had been for the last three years. My pay was cut by nearly $20,000, and I was the primary income earner within our household. This was the last thing we needed to happen while we were struggling with adapting to marriage. All I could think about was how much easier things would be if you were making more money, but I was the one that encouraged you to avoid 9-5 jobs and focus on growing in the field of your desire. This had to be the darkest period of our marriage. The mortgage began to fall behind. Both car notes became delinquent, and your car was repossessed for a few weeks. The cable had to be cut canceled, and our auto insurance coverage lapsed. My 401k was almost empty. I could barely afford to feed us. Worst of all, we began to blame each other for unfulfilled marital expectations. It really seemed like we were not going to be able to overcome these problems, but something turned this all around.

After long discussions, help from family and lots of prayer, you and I decided to make this marriage work in despite of the obstacles we faced. We sought counseling and made some important changes that would turn out to be imperative to our future. Instead of folding to our financial problems, you enrolled in a program at Aveda Institute and continued to pursue a career in beauty, while I worked on increasing my salary at work. We also made a mutual decision to no longer hold onto the biggest financial strain on our wallets by pursuing a short sale. Getting rid of the first house I ever purchased wasn't easy, but it was necessary for us to quickly recover from our financial hardships. I realized that I had to take a few steps back to ensure you wouldn't have to give up on your dreams. You were just beginning your career, while I was pretty established for someone a few years shy of thirty. We needed to start fresh to ensure both of our lifestyle dreams could be achieved, and with that said, it was time to move back into an apartment. This sacrifice only strengthened our relationship. You knew I would do whatever it took to ensure our future financial stability and began to truly trust me as a husband. It was at this moment that I realized our marriage would only grow stronger. We both invested more into each other's dreams and ignored the expectations of society. We didn't need to live in a house with a white picket fence to believe we were a success. Within three months of downsizing our lifestyle, our cash flow began to increase. Not having the pressure of a mortgage payment eased all of our financial burdens. We paid the car loans off, collections bills were paid off, and I obtained a new position which increased our household income. We were on a roll. To make matters even better, within the next year, you finished school and began working as an esthetician and makeup artist. It only took one year for us to be debt free. We were back on our feet, and it wouldn't have happened if we didn't agree to follow the same financial plan. Being dedicated to pursuing our dreams and eliminating our debt was paying off, but another unexpected benefit grew from this experience.

Before experiencing these hardships with you, I was dedicated to rising up the ladder in corporate America. I wasn't thinking about helping others overcome their own debt problems, and certainly wasn't thinking about writing a book. Your pursuit of a fulfilling career in which you loved inspired me to focus more on doing the things I loved, which was helping others. My job provided me with all the tools I needed to understand the ends and outs of personal finance, and it allowed me to engage with thousands of people experiencing financial hardships. Hearing their stories and learning more about the lifestyles of people outside of my community, which were top one percent income earners and the bottom twenty-five percent, taught me a lot about consumer credit and overcoming money-related problems. All I needed was a little direction, and you inspired it. Coming from where we come from, people don't write books and lead financial lectures. Our families weren't filled with people that stepped out of the norm to pursue something bigger than them. This is why I know that none of the books I wrote would have ever been written without your inspiration. You've taught me to be more than just a provider and marital partner. You proved to me that it is possible to build a financially compatible household, and accomplish things previously thought to be impossible. Mrs. Lorick, I love you, and thank you for helping me to become the husband you need and a leader in our community.

Contents

INTRODUCTION

What do lifestyle goals, dreams, aspirations, career goals, and desires all have in common? They're typically developed before our first real date. I'm not referring to the one time we went out to see a movie with a high school crush or the time we went to the eighth grade social with the first person that asked or said yes. I'm talking about the date without a curfew or parental guidance-better known as an adult date. Our first adult date takes place after we've developed an understanding of personal finance. Due to the sequence of these events, we are challenged with the task of overcoming one of the biggest obstacles to creating long-lasting relationships: financial compatibility. Some of us believe love will conquer all, but if that were true, the divorce rate would be a lot lower. The truth is that financial compatibility influences the likelihood of maintaining long-term relationships, and the concept of love is often misinterpreted.

The love that can overcome financial instability requires sacrifice, pain, suffering, humility, and a lack of conditions. This type of love is called agape love, and it is rarely obtained during the first ten years of marriage. Displaying such a high level of selfless love, while constantly being influenced by society to be self-absorbed is quite a difficult task. Therefore, we need something to help us maintain our relationships until we are able to display agape love. This is where financial compatibility comes into the picture. Individuals who are able to overcome their different concepts of financial success and create mutually beneficial lifestyles will typically form a bond that fortifies strong relationships. Those who aren't able to do this often become another number in rising divorcee or newly single family home statistics.

Understanding this reality has led me to writing this book. While the first book may have touched on this topic, this edition covers its complexities. Whether you are single or married, this book will add value to your life, and help you build stronger financial compatibility with the people you love. All that is required is an open-mind and humble heart.

1

IT ALL BEGINS WITH YOU

Before you can become a part of a financially compatible relationship, you must first understand how to find the right person, and how to build compatibility. Too often; people begin these searches by creating unreasonable expectations of others, and this is where the majority of financial compatibility issues are born. Some women and men expect their partners to earn a six-figure salary simply because he or she has a master's degree or doctor of philosophy ("PhD"). Others believe rich parent's guarantee's a wealthy lifestyle. Some people can't even understand how another person's credit score could sink below 630 without an extreme case of fiscal irresponsibility. Financial expectations like these are created for others without consideration of the environmental factors that lead to the financial decision. Simple factors such as family habits, community structure, education system, and religion greatly contribute to individual financial values, but selfish desires cause people to ignore them while evaluating others. These actions ruin efforts to successfully identify compatible lovers by increasing the chances of choosing incompatible mates. They also hinder the growth of long-term relationships; like marriages. While overcoming a financially incompatible relationship is difficult, it is possible to increase compatibility when the correct steps are taken. The same holds true for single adults looking for love. In both cases, getting a better understanding of oneself from a financial perspective is where the search for financial compatibility should begin. The best way to gain this insight is to start with a self-evaluation.

To begin the evaluation, you need to go to a place where it is possible to escape distractions. This place can be inside or outside your home, but make sure nobody will bother you. For those of you who are parents, I realize this may seem like mission impossible, but it can be done. Try staying in the car an extra fifteen minutes or parking around the corner if your home isn't an option. Once you're in this place, close your eyes and begin to think back to your childhood experiences. Try to recall your first encounter with money and the early financial lessons you learned from your parents. These memories will typically involve moments where you wanted something and realized one or both of your parents had to spend money or leave the home to fulfill your request. The object you desired may have been a toy or game that you consistently clamored over. Your parents' response to your persistent request helped to create one of your first financial lessons. For some, your parents' responded with a "yes" and purchased the item of your desires. Others parents said "no" and explained how they couldn't afford to purchase it, which helped to usher in the idea of a limited money supply. Whichever way this interaction played out, you learned something from it, and received your first lesson in personal finance. Following this event, you probably began to pay more attention to the financial habits of your parents and family members. When your older siblings purchased some candy from the store, you noticed how much money they spent. Trips to the local market began to teach you about your parents' shopping habits. Try your best to remember these types of observations. While you may think they are insignificant, these moments created the foundation of your concept of money. Several published studies have shown that we develop most of our personality between ages one and eight, and this includes your attitude towards finances.

What were your parents showing you through their habits? What did you learn from your siblings and close family members? Did you learn anything while watching television and listening to music? Everything from the environment you were raised in contributes to your beliefs about money, and recalling these experiences is essential to your self-evaluation. Get a notepad and write down any reoccurring themes from these memories. If you only come up with a few, don't attempt to artificially create more. You must be completely honest for this process to work correctly. Title this list, "Childhood Lessons", and put it to the side once you've completed it. For the next stage of this self-evaluation, you'll need to move further up memory lane and recall events from your teenage years.

As teens, we begin to separate ourselves from the beliefs of our parents and take on other ideas about life. Our friends and school environment become a lot more influential during this period of our lives, and we tend to stray away from values learned at home. This change creates an opportunity to learn good and bad financial habits. Think back to this time in your life and try to recall the financial lessons you learned during these years. What classes did you take in high school that caused you do think differently about the economy and personal finance? What common financial themes could be found in the music you loved or the television shows you faithfully watched? Don't forget about the impact your friends had on you. How did they feel about money, class, and poverty? Did you often share their views? If not, I highly doubt the people you are thinking about were true friends. It is more likely that you are thinking about associates or other teens you admired. Real friends are rarely total opposites, and they likely influenced a lot of your decision making. Try hard to remember what you and your friends thought about money around this time period. Make a note of any reoccurring themes that come to mind. If you're experiencing difficulties recalling these moments, try to focus on your previous thoughts about education, cost, and adult -lifestyle expenses. How did these lessons affect your outlook on adult life? Did the idea of paying your own bills and student loans discourage or encourage you to pursue adulthood? These are the years that fears related to adulthood are fully formed. Most teens want adult independence, but without the bills and boring lifestyle. For some, this feeling will persist for a lifetime, and these individuals may never truly grasp the concept of financial responsibility. However, some teens are pushed to prepare for the financial responsibilities that accompany adulthood. They decide to choose career paths that are the most financially lucrative, and they often avoid situations that could lead to financial hardship like having unprotected sex. Use these memories to help you recall the ideas that helped to shape your concept of personal finance, and record them under a new list titled, "Teenage Lessons."

By the time you are twenty-one, your ideas about money and the values that drive your financial decision are fully formed. While there is room for slight adjustments, most of these ideas will remain in place. Your money personality has been developed, and understanding it will help you choose more compatible companions. What exactly is a money personality? It is a combination of consistent responses to financial decision-making conditions based on individual values. These values will typically align with the themes on your lists. Use them as a guide while attempting to identify your money personality.

Though there are several ways to describe a money personality, most people fall under one of these dominant money personality classifications: chaser, builder, manager, or victim. The next page contains a brief description of each dominant money personality. Read them over and determine which one best matches your financial behavior, and aligns with your lists. Keep in mind you may relate to several of these classifications, but typically one is more dominant than the others.

Chaser

Chasers are people who consistently attempt to acquire more wealth than someone else. These individuals perceive life as a race where first place is the only winner. This results in more financial risks being taken. They determine their level of success based on the failures of others. They also have a high regard for social status. The financial aspects of the lifestyles of people like Bill Gates and Warren Buffet are used as a barometer of success. They may often be heard saying, "I haven't made it because I'm still not on the level of..." People with this money personality will relocate more often than others. Their insistence on social advancement will not allow them to live in one setting for a long period of time.

Builder

Builders desire to increase everything they acquire. These individuals may be considered rich, but want to expand their assets as much as possible. They perceive life as an individual race with the goal of beating an ever changing best time. They may often be heard using the phrase, "I am working to expand my empire." These individual are semi-stable, but relocate more often than managers or victims.

Managers

Managers desire to manage their earnings to the best of their ability. Income level is not a major concern. They are inspired to advance in their career, but not solely for the purpose of earning more money. Preparation and effort are highly regarded values to manager personalities. They use phrases like, "As long as I do my part everything else will fall in place." These people are less likely to frequently relocate and usually live a more stable lifestyle.

Victims

Victims consistently blame their personal failures on others and circumstances. These individuals are not willing to do what it takes to change their circumstances. They often perceive life as a fixed race and feel cheating is necessary for victory. You may often hear them say, "It's not my fault." They are semi-risky partners because of their lack of desire to change. Victims may complain about their lifestyle, but will not take advantage of good opportunities. These habits make victims a difficult spouse to live with. To determine if living with a victim is possible, you must understand the compatibility of these dispositions.

Once you've identified your dominant money personality, link it to one of the following secondary money personalities: controller, follower, or teammate.

Controller

A controller is exactly what you would expect. A person who needs to control the family finances. This person refuses to follow anyone else's lead when it comes to financial matters, but is not always the best person to lead. Part of a controller's reasoning for his or her actions can usually be tied to college and professional accomplishments. Controllers are also willing to make the tough decisions when others are not.

Follower

Followers are those who don't want to lead when it comes to financial matters. They'd rather sit in the background and either offer advice or point out the deficiencies of others. While it may seem like people with this secondary money personality have inferior money-management skills, this is not always true. The desire to avoid leadership doesn't equate to a lack of financial literacy; it only means these individuals are more comfortable as followers.

Teammate

Teammates do whatever it takes to get the job done. They will lead when needed and follow when asked. People with this secondary money personality are not afraid to criticize their partner's financial decisions, but they are also willing to applaud great decisions. They are not in the relationship to only say the things people want to hear. They are only concerned with the well-being of the relationship. The only dominant money personality that is impossible to co-exist with a secondary teammate money personality is a victim. By definition, victims are looking to blame others, which is in direct opposition to the teammate personality.

Now that you've identified your dominant and secondary money personalities, compare them to your lists. Your Childhood Lessons list, Teenage Lessons list, and money personalities should all correlate. When they don't, either something drastic has occurred between your childhood and adulthood that has caused a paradigm shift, or it is possible that you need to look a little harder for correlations. No matter the reason for this occurrence, move forward with this exercise anyway. If you're not happy with the results, don't run away from them. Embrace your financial values and improve in the areas that make you cringe. Knowing yourself only makes you a better love partner, and you will need this knowledge to move forward with finding and growing financial compatibility.

2

THE SINGLE LIFE: SINGLE AND LOOKING

So you're ready to begin the search for a new companion and want to know where to start. I'm sure you've thought about the qualities you'd prefer in a potential lover, but what do you do next? I would suggest creating a few mechanisms to help you distinguish the winners from the losers. However, one stumbling block to doing this successfully is dishonest behavior.

People are excellent actors during the first couple of dates, and some have the ability to keep this act going for several years. This ability makes it very difficult to accurately assess personal morals during the beginning stages of dating; therefore, you should focus your efforts on evaluating something that can't be hidden so easily: their financial habits. We may be able to hide the bad experiences that stick with us from previous relationships. We can even hide unattractive social dysfunctions that exist within our family or friendship circles. But we can't completely hide our financial habits from each other. Even the best con artists are only capable of hiding the secrets of their financial habits for a few weeks before being ousted by those paying close attention. To become an expert at gathering this helpful information, you must first learn how to recognize the signs that will reveal their financial habits.

Tool #1: The Covert Examination

There is nothing worse than having to answer 1,000 questions about your life during the first date. Nobody enjoys being put on the examination table by a complete stranger or friend, much less on the first date. The early stages of dating are meant to be informative, yet enjoyable, and coming off like an investigator will send most people running for the hills. The key to getting the information you need without becoming a nuisance is to ask a few precise questions. Once you get past the easy questions about their family structure, home life, career, and goals, use these questions to gain better insight about their financial well-being. Here are a few questions to ask on your first date:

How long have you been living in this area?

What you are looking for with this question are signs of stability. Most creditors consider frequent movers a higher credit risk than those who remain in one area for several years, and you should too. Active military personnel, professional athletes, artist (actors, musicians, etc.), and a few other careers require lots of travel, but most people don't have this issue. Frequent relocation requires reestablishment, and why would someone need to do this so often? Outside of relocation needs created by the previously mentioned career types, the likely cause can be traced back to some personal financial motives. Those financial motives will not be fully determined by this one question, but it does help to reveal a hint of some level of a need for change from a financial perspective. Secondary and tertiary questions regarding frequent relocating will eventually reveal more about their financial habits, but they can be saved for other dates or just another time. If you do chose to move further along this path during the first date, proceed with caution or this may be the last date.

How often do you get to take a vacation, and where have you traveled?

What you are looking for with this question is simple: financial capabilities. People experiencing financial hardships are less likely to travel than their counterparts. Follow up this question by asking if he or she has any pictures from these vacations. It's easy to say you take yearly or semi-annual vacations, but proving it requires evidence. If he or she doesn't have pictures, don't make it a big deal. At some point, these pictures have to turn up in their home or on social networking websites. If the pictures don't surface within a few weeks, he or she is probably lying. In this day and age, it is very rare to find someone that travels but never takes any pictures. Camera phones make this task too easy, and if they don't have a cell phone, you should be a little concerned.

What kind of cell phone do you have?

This may seem like a silly question, but the answers will let you know something about their finances. Most adults in the United States own a cell phone, and the age of this device says a lot about the owner. The major service providers offer free upgrades to long-term customers, so why would someone be carrying a four- to five- year old cellular device? Sure, they could be very conservative, but the free and newer cellular devices which accompany contract extensions are more user-friendly. Adults over the age of fifty can get a pass on this one, but it's still something to think about. You should also be concerned if he or she uses a prepaid or government-issued cell phone. While I am sure there are people in the United States with great, elaborate explanations for carrying a prepaid cell phone, good reasons are far and few between. Not only is it less expensive to have a mobile phone with a contract, but it's also normal.

These are just a few questions that can be asked to give you clues about the financial status of the person you're dating, but paying attention to his or her dating persona will offer you much more information.

What is a dating persona? It is a description of someone's consistent dating habits. This includes dating locations, common personality traits, spending habits, and other frequent, observable actions that are taken during a date. Once you understand how to interpret these habits, you will have the clues needed to determine financial compatibility. Review all the dating personas listed in this chapter, and see if they remind you of someone you've dated or are dating.

The Hopeless Romantic

Have you ever gone out with someone that attempts to make the moment bigger than what it is? That person has a high probability of being a hopeless romantic. These individuals consistently attempt to make each date a romantic scene straight out of the latest popular love story. They don't wait until Valentine's Day or a special occasion to display their perfection of romanticism. Their efforts will be consistent. This persona isn't for those that are romantic once per month. I am referring to individuals that display this behavior on a weekly basis. They see every date as an opportunity to woo their love interest. Anyone with this dating style is either well-off financially or attempting to portray someone with great wealth. The best way to distinguish between the two is to carefully look for inconsistencies with this behavior over a period of time. A con artist won't be able to keep this act up for more than a few months. True hopeless romantics are more consistent. Here is a short story that describes what life could be like when dating someone with this dating persona:

Jordan met Skylar at a work function two weeks ago, and they both seemed interested in each other. After a few days and several lunch dates, they decided to start dating. Jordan told Skylar not to worry about any of the details regarding their first date and only requested Skylar wear something nice and upscale. Skylar agreed to this arrangement and was very pleased with the idea of not having to take the lead. Once the planning was done and the date night arrived, Skylar was ready for whatever the night would bring. Jordan showed up at Skylar's house dressed to impress, and they both were in awe of each other's appearance. As they got into Jordan's Mercedes, Skylar asks where they were headed, but Jordan wouldn't reveal their destination. Jordan only reminded Skylar not to worry, and promised an extraordinary night. They eventually arrived at one of the finest five-star restaurants in their hometown and were immediately seated at a reserved table. This table had everything. There were candles, a bottle of champagne, fine silverware, flowers, and a dedicated waiter. As the waiter handed them the menus, Jordan let Skylar know that price was not a problem and anything on the menu could be chosen. Skylar then proceeded to choose a moderately priced meal, but Jordan suggested a more expensive meal based on past experiences. Skylar went ahead with Jordan's suggestion and also ordered a recommended appetizer. As the night went on, they talked and enjoyed their meals, but Jordan revealed more plans for their date. Jordan had purchased two tickets to see a popular comedian at a comedy club that was few blocks away from the restaurant. After they finished desert, Jordan paid the bill with tip. The valet bought the car to the front of the restaurant, and they got in and drove a few blocks to the comedy club. Once they made it to the club, Jordan pulled out two back-stage passes to meet the superstar comedian after the show. Skylar couldn't believe all of this was happening on their first date, but was enjoying everything. They watched the comedian perform for about an hour from their front row seats and proceeded to the backstage area to meet him after the show. Once backstage, Skylar and Jordan talked to the comedian for a few minutes and left with two autographed photos. Once they arrived at Skylar's house, Jordan walked Skylar to the door and asked if they could go out again sometime in the near future. Skylar agreed, and they began to enjoy nights like this for the next several months.

Jordan paid for everything and always reminded Skylar that there was no expectation for repayment in any form, but then it happened. Skylar had been driving the same old Buick for the last ten years, and it drove its last mile. The engine died, and Skylar had to get a new car. After doing some online searches, Skylar found a great deal for a desirable car. It was a three year old Lexus and available at a local dealership for $3,000 cheaper than anywhere else. Skylar didn't want to go to the dealership alone, and decided to invite Jordan to ride along. Once they arrived to the dealership, a car salesman greeted them and immediately made his way to the car Skylar desired. After doing a quick walk around and test drive, the time had come to decide if a purchase would be made. Jordan was pretty quiet during the test drive, but suddenly became very vocal. Skylar was ready to purchase the car, but Jordan wouldn't let it happen. Jordan wanted to handle all of the negotiations and didn't approve of the deal Skylar was willing to accept. Though Skylar researched the market value of this car and knew the deal was great, Jordan felt the need to handle this affair. The cat was officially out the bag. While Jordan spoiled Skylar with lavish evenings filled with good food and great experiences, it all came with a price. When it came to financial affairs, Jordan wanted to control everything, which left Skylar with a choice to make: stay in this relationship knowing all financial matters must be handled by Jordan or leave it alone.

If you're dating someone like Jordan, make sure his or her charming ways don't distract you from reality. All the nice gestures usually come with certain financial stipulations. Many hopeless romantics expect their mates to allow them to have a lot of control within the relationship. Money is often used as a method of controlling others, and this dating persona has a high propensity to be accompanied by a controlling nature. These habits tend to remain during marriage, and if you aren't prepared to deal with this now, don't expect things to get easier as the relationship progresses. These hopeless romantics will likely want to handle the finances and expect you to follow their lead.

The Perpetrator

Most people don't reveal their true personality for the first couple of dates, but the "perpetrator" actually attempts to hide who he or she is for longer periods of time. These individuals use dates as opportunities to create a new character and live out the lifestyle of others. The best way to identify a perpetrator is to follow the money instead of the stories. Their spending habits typically won't match the persona they are trying to sell. Perpetrators will frequently offer numerous excuses to cover up their lack of consistent behavior. He or she will be able to afford an expensive night on the town one week and won't be able to see you again for several weeks. They need to space out their dates to remain consistent and lessen the chance of a blown cover. Covering up lies is their top priority, and you will always come second or worse.

What can these behaviors tell you about their financial habits? Sadly, there is very little to learn because of their habitual lies. However, there is one fact that remains true about all perpetrators: they spend a lot of money on efforts to cover up their lies. While using money to strengthen dishonesty doesn't guarantee financial stability or instability, it does reveal spending habits. All money spent to cover up lies is simply a waste because the truth will come out at some point. If they lie about who they are, expect them to lie about their finances too. Only commit to long-term relationships with these characters if you have little concern for financial matters.

The Ham

A ham is a person who consistently feels the need to be the center of attention. They want to make date night all about their own glorification. Individuals with this dating persona will typically spend large sums of money to make themselves look better. Sometimes this includes spending money on you just to be able to brag about their efforts.

If you think it will be hard to identify a ham, you are sadly mistaken. Because of their need to be in the spotlight, hams are not hard to find. Here is a short story that describes what life could be like when dating someone with this dating persona:

Jaime and Chandler were dating and spending every weekend together for the past three months. These weekend dates typically involved eating, drinking, and dancing, but Jamie wanted to do something different this coming Saturday. Jamie asked Chandler if they could attend a friend's party instead of sticking to their usual routine. He agreed, but request to drive his own car to the event. This request didn't seem like a big deal, so Jaime agreed. The Friday night before the party, Chandler called Jamie to find out what she planned on wearing to the party. Jamie shared this information and then reminded Chandler that the party begins at 10 p.m., so they wouldn't arrive late. Chandler assured Jamie they would arrive on time and have fun at the party. The next evening, around

9:45 p.m., Jamie was dressed and ready to leave, but Chandler hadn't arrived. The expectations of this date were already set, so there was no reason for him to be late. Five minutes later, Jamie called Chandler to find out what was going on, but there was no answer. He eventually arrived to pick Jamie up around 10:15 p.m., and offered some lame excuse about needing to get gas as his reason for being late. Once they were on the road, Jamie noticed Chandler was wearing expensive jewelry and his car was detailed. While it is normal for Chandler to dress nicely, that night things seemed a little over the top. They finally made it to the party around 11 p.m. Chandler dropped Jamie off at the door as he searched for a parking spot. Jamie walked into her friend's house, and after ten minutes passed, realized Chandler hadn't come inside after dropping her off. After another five minutes passed, he finally entered the house and immediately started mingling with everyone, before attempting to find Jamie. She hadn't noticed that Chandler was inside the house, and began looking for him, but was suddenly distracted by a group of people huddled around someone talking loudly. Jamie moved closer to the crowd to see what was going on and discovered the loud person was Chandler. He was telling jokes about work and seemed to be having a great time, while Jamie was left feeling abandoned. Chandler didn't seem the least bit interested in what she was doing. Jamie expected to enjoy this party with Chandler, but they hardly interacted the entire night. When the party was coming to an end, Jamie was ready to go home, but Chandler refused to leave. He was having too good of a time to leave and wanted to stay a little longer, which further upset Jamie. After Jamie asked if they could leave a few more times, Chandler finally agreed, and they left the party. Once they were in the car, Chandler noticed Jamie was a little upset and asked if she had a good time. Jamie was really disappointed that Chandler wasn't around her much and told him about those feelings. Chandler looked Jamie directly in her eyes and said, "I thought you would appreciate me being the life of the party. I'm sure your friends loved me and are looking forward to hanging out again." This explanation only further annoyed Jamie, and she then realized what she had gotten herself into. Chandler was a ham, and she couldn't remain in a relationship with him. He was demoted to the friend zone, before he even knew it happened.

While being a ham doesn't guarantee financial prosperity or ruin, it's easy to predict where most of their money goes. They typically like to be in control of their money and are not too concerned about anyone else's financial well-being. Don't expect these individuals to invest in your dreams and aspirations. Hams are all about themselves, and you are typically just a trophy on their mantle. Unless you are satisfied with simply being a part of someone else's dreams or being with someone that has no interest in your financial situation, you may want to avoid anyone like this.

The Mogul

Moguls are like hams that are focused on financial prominence. They want to be recognized for the empire they're building and won't let anyone slow down their progress. Expensive and extravagant dates are their tools for building self-worth and confidence. They wouldn't dare be seen in a low-budget restaurant or inexpensive clothing store. If you're dating a mogul, everything about their lifestyle will scream success. Five-star hotels and private beaches are a requirement for their vacations. Their children must also have the best clothes, toys, and education. Public schools are frowned upon and rarely good enough for their kids. If the people you're dating don't express those views, there are other ways to tell if he or she is a mogul. Moguls never or rarely allow you to pay for a meal. They see this as an insult to their stature and feel belittled by your perceived attempt of establishing financial equality. When it comes to long-term relationships, moguls like to handle all the finances, and if you're not prepared to let someone else handle your money, run away. These individuals are big spenders and don't mix well with conservative spenders.

The Damsel in Distress

Don't let the name of this dating persona fool you, Damsels can be male or female. These serial daters are always looking for someone to upgrade their lifestyle. They rarely want to pay for anything and always have an excuse for their lack of social progression. The reasons for this behavior can often be traced back to their childhood, and without professional help, these individuals will never overcome their victim mentality. If you plan on starting a long-term relationship with a damsel, be prepared to handle all the finances. Damsels' are rarely good money managers and will always depend on others to fix their financial problems.

The Even Steven

An even steven is someone who demands his or her relationships to be mutually beneficial. They will not pay for every date or allow you to always pay. Their ideal relationships consist of two people who are fully capable of self-reliance. During the holidays, they will base their gift giving on the capabilities of their partners. If you can only afford a small gift, their gifts will be modest, and vice versa. Even stevens rarely take big financial risks. They fear the possibility of living check-to-check and won't let anyone put them in a position to experience financial hardships. If you are dating someone like this, you can expect him or her to be tedious a money manager. While many people may seem like an even steven, the best way to distinguish between the real and fake is to pay attention to their relationships with family members and friends.

Authentic even stevens don't limit these behaviors to dating partners, they require this from everyone. If you plan on creating a long-term relationship with an even steven, make sure you are dedicated to fiscal responsibility.

The Explorer

An explorer is someone who is open to conventional and unique dating experiences. They enjoy both eating out at a low-budget restaurant and sharing meals at local five-star restaurants. The only thing that bothers them about dating is a lack of diversity. They need consistent change to remain happy and are willing to spend their money to prevent constant boredom. This desire for diversity doesn't necessarily equate to a need for multiple dating partners, but it typically requires their dating partners to be very open-minded. Explorers are open to paying for meals, splitting bills, and allowing others to cover the cost of a night out on the town. They also don't mind last-minute changes to planned dates if those changes are for the purpose of creating an enjoyable experience. This behavior is typically not limited to their dating habits. A close examination of their wardrobe will also reflect this need for diversity. An explorers closet must be filled with clothes to fit a variety of experiences. Their vehicles will also vary. One night he or she will pull out the driveway in the BMW and the next night in the Ford Focus. Having so many options requires steady income, but don't be fooled into thinking this guarantees financial security. Explorers are not too keen on paying attention to details and are not fans of structure. Without the assistance of a partner with good money management skills, they will overlook some of the long -term costs associated with having a good time. If you plan on creating a long-term relationship with an explorer, be prepared to be a good money manager. Your explorer will need you to make sure he or she doesn't spend too much money chasing fun, but this task shouldn't be too difficult. They are usually willing to step aside and let you handle the finances once they trust your money management skills.

The Homebody

If you're an active dater, I'm certain you've dated a homebody. This was the guy or girl who consistently preferred to stay home over going out for date night. They view nights out on the town as a luxury and will stay home whenever the option is given. While they will offer several reasons for wanting to stay in the house, financial concerns are the typical culprit. These concerns can be traced back to financial hardships or a frugal nature. People experiencing financial hardships can't afford the costs of frequent out-of -home dates, but affordability is not a common issue for frugal-natured individuals. Your job is to figure out which reason relates to the person you are dating. If he or she prefers to stay home because of a frugal nature, be prepared to deal with a penny-pinching money manager. He or she will likely insist on handling all financial affairs when committing to a long-term, monogamous relationship. On the other hand, if the person you're dating stays home because of financial problems, you need to know the severity of these issues. Long-term problems can usually be traced back to bad financial habits, but short-term problems can be caused by an endless number of reasons. Don't be afraid to ask about these issues if you're dating a homebody. The answers to your questions could determine if you're financially compatible. Homebodies with serious financial problems may be a great match for moguls, and hopeless romantics, but most others are not compatible with these individuals.

The Saint

People that use religious beliefs to define the parameters of their dating relationships fall under this dating persona. If the religion they are following teaches that all dating should be conducted in a group or family setting, they won't take part in one-on-one dating. When they are taught that men should pay for all meals, anything else will seem inappropriate. They eat, sleep, and live for their spiritual beliefs and financial matters are not exempt. If you plan on developing a long-term relationship with a saint, be sure to gain a good understanding of their religious beliefs. Religion usually trumps any other beliefs, and you need to be sure you can deal with their practices.

The Group Dater

If you've ever dated someone who prefers to date in a group setting, he or she falls under this dating persona. The group dater loves to be around people, but hates one-on-one dating. They will take you to a party or gathering with friends, but refuse to partake in a candle light dinner with you. When they come to visit you, a friend is always present. Everything about their behavior screams scandalous and fun at the same time. This also can be said for their financial habits. Habitual group daters don't want to spend one-on-one time with you and rarely will be open about their financial matters. While you can pay close attention to their living arrangement and spending habits, they will not allow you to get close enough to see the whole picture. I'm not sure if you should entertain the idea of a long-term relationship with someone so secretive, but if you choose to proceed, don't expect him or her to ever be an open book. People don't typically change this type of behavior just because they are in a committed relationship. They like to keep some secrets, and you need to be content with not knowing everything about their finances if you plan on staying with them. The reasons for their secretive ways can range from cheating to religious beliefs, but figuring that out could take years.

The Club and Bar Junkie

Every once in a while, you are bound to run into someone who loves to take you out to local clubs and bars. These club hoppers don't care for expensive restaurants or fancy dinner parties. They love to party hard as if they are still in college or just turning 21. This isn't your occasional once-a-month club goer. These individuals feel the need to go clubbing or bar hopping every weekend, and also expect their love interest to come along. During my late teens and early twenties, people like this were my favorite dating partners, but I despised them by my mid-twenties. Sure, they were fun to hang out with, but frequently embarrassing at the same time. Of all the club junkies I dated, one stands out more than any others. For the sake of her privacy, I'll just refer to her as Candy. She was quite a beautiful woman. Candy was about 5 '6" with a smooth, but radiant caramel skin tone. Her walk demanded the attention of all onlookers because of her subtle hip movement and elegant stride. She wasn't skinny, but far from what most people would call thick. If I had to guess, I would say she weighed about 130 pounds and had a Megan Goode type of figure. On top of all her physical attractive traits, she was very intelligent. Candy was an accounting major at a local university and rarely settled for any grades less than a B. But while she was a great student during the day, she was a regular partier at night. We met through a mutual friend and instantly connected. We could talk for hours about our experiences in Baltimore and college. Like myself, she was from Baltimore and a first generation college kid, and these similarities led to great conversations. We eventually started dating, and everything was great. Candy and I went to a club or two about once or twice a month, but mostly ate out at local restaurants. About three months into our dating relationship, things began to change. Candy told me she was getting tired of going out to restaurants and wanted to go clubbing more often. I disagreed, but tried to make it work. We went back and forth about her need to go clubbing every week, and eventually I had to end our dating relationship. There were no hard feelings, but I was a bit disappointed. I couldn't believe such an intelligent and beautiful woman felt the need to go to the club so much, but that's who she was, and I wasn't looking to marry her anyway. Eight or nine years later, I was driving through downtown Baltimore and saw Candy again, leaving the same club she frequented in her early twenties. I was coming back in town from a quick vacation and couldn't believe what I was seeing. She was now thirty and still going to the same clubs, doing the same things. Maybe she was working at the club, or maybe this was a one-time celebration. I can't be sure why she was there, but I surely didn't see many other thirty-year-old adults there. This club was still known as a hopper club or a place for people in their late teens and early twenties. While I'm sure there is someone out there who is willing to form a long-term relationship with someone like Candy, I wasn't that guy. She may have moved on to have a successful career as an accountant and even created a beautiful family, but in my mind she still was a club junkie, and not a match for anyone like myself.

When it comes to spending money, most club and bar junkies are willing to pay a high price for anything that leads to intoxication. Some may even be ragging alcoholics, but not all. You should expect people with this dating persona to invest heavily in the pursuit of a good time. Some will be bad money managers and others will be fiscal wizards, but almost all will make sure there is room in the budget for partying. If you have a problem with people spending money that could be invested in stocks and bonds on alcohol, pills, and partying, don't plan on creating a long-term relationship with these club and bar junkies. Conservative money managers need not apply.

The Cheapskate

Cheapskates view dating as an obstacle more than an opportunity to spend quality time with someone. They refuse to pay full price for any activity and constantly look for the cheapest ways to satisfy the people they're dating. If they take you to a five-star restaurant, there must be some huge discount or promotion involved. The cars they drive are typically hanging on for dear life or are a break down away from ending up in the junk yard. The clothes they wear reflect the sales and clearance rack of most major department stores. When cheapskates tip, they never offer more than eight to twelve percent of the bill. These masters of frugality constantly look for ways to avoid paying full price for anything, but their behavior doesn't necessarily mean they are broke. Many cheapskates are very good money managers and earn over six figures annually. While assuming these people are broke or wealthy may be a mistake, there are some safe assumptions you can make. It is safe to say that most cheapskates are very diligent money managers. People that tend to display occasional frugality are not cheapskates and may simply be experiencing temporary financial hardships. On the other hand, cheapskates remain frugal through good and bad times. They are consistently cheap and maintaining this behavior requires diligent money management skills. If you plan on creating a long-term relationship with a cheapskate, make sure you're ready to be criticized for your lack of money management skills. While they may not handle all the money, they will be critical of how it's used.

The Sports Fan

It's Friday night and your new dating friend gives you a call. He or she offers you the opportunity to attend a local sporting event. It seems like it will be fun, so you agree to go along. The evening goes well, and you decide to spend more time with this person in the future. The next four to five dates with this person go along the same script, and you suddenly realize that you are dating the sports fan. When you're dealing with these sports fanatics, nearly every date is centered around their favorite sports teams. Their closets are filled with sports paraphernalia. Their homes are decorated with shrines to their favorite athlete's, and their emotions are tied to the success or lack of success of their favorite teams. These are die-hard fanatics, and dating them means accepting their love for sports. It also means a good portion of their income will be spent in support of their favorite teams. They can't go without their season tickets and frequently fly out of town whenever their favorite teams are on the road. If they are forced to choose between going to an autograph signing and spending quality time with a potential lover, they will usually choose the first option. If you are planning on starting a long-term relationship with these folks, you must be okay with these spending habits. He or she is very likely to be sticklers for handling his or her own finances. They won't trust their ability to support their teams in your hands and need to control their own finances. They also won't allow your financial habits to keep them from being a sports fanatic.

The Serial Dater

Serial daters are people that refuse to be alone and consistently seek companionship immediately after ending a relationship. They rarely enter into long-term, committed relationships because of their constant need for change. This behavior can typically be traced to some childhood issues and is very difficult to abandon. Because of their need for constant change, serial daters are often inconsistent money managers. They must become big spenders to please their needy dating partners. When dating frugal individuals, they become tedious money managers. Serial daters are truly the chameleons of the dating world. With so much change taking place, it can be difficult to discover their deep-rooted financial principles.

In fact, serial daters change their financial habits so frequently they easily forget the childhood financial lessons which shaped their understanding of money. If these individuals ever decide to settle down into a long-term relationship, it will be difficult for them to conform to more consistent financial habits. Their partners must be willing to work with them through these changes for the relationship to succeed. Serial daters are not comfortable with letting others control their finances; therefore, their partners will need to be patient and very understanding. Anyone not willing to work through these changes should leave serial daters alone; unless there is a preference for drama-filled, tumultuous relationships.

The Race Baiter

Race baiters choose their dating partners based on racial background. They refuse to date anyone outside of a particular race and rarely ever make exceptions. It doesn't matter if their racial preferences make up the minority or majority populous of a particular region. These folk are dead set on dating people from particular ethnic backgrounds. The reasons for their preference will vary, but all can be traced back to prejudicial beliefs. These beliefs drive them to seek out dating partners based on assumptions. When race baiters expect their partners to be poor, they are disappointed when the opposite is true. Their partners need to match up with their prejudice beliefs because they don't like surprises and refuse to adjust to unexpected behaviors. Because of this desire for predictable behavior, race baiters can easily be identified. They flee relationships at the first sign of any challenges to their beliefs and run towards individuals that match up to their expectations. The lack of compliance to their assumptions upsets them, and they can't hide these frustrations. The opposite is also true. They always celebrate confirmation of prejudice beliefs. A discussion about their previous dating partners and preferences will also reveal how much they hold onto their prejudice beliefs. Keep in mind that we all hold on to some racial prejudices, but these individuals build their lives around them. How does this relate to their financial habits? Race baiters like stability. That doesn't necessarily equate to being a good money manager, but their behavior will be consistent. If these individuals are gamblers, they will always be gamblers. Race baiters that are great money managers will rarely experience financial missteps. These are people who don't like change because their confidence is tied to being able to predict human behavior. If you are dating someone with this dating persona, expect him or her to desire your compliance with racial prejudices. If you can't handle living up to their beliefs, run the other way. All people are capable of change, but racial prejudice often remains intact for a lifetime.

The Dedicated Employee

Have you ever dated someone who can't seem to escape their job? Remember the guy or girl who wouldn't stop talking about work and seemed to be married to his or her job? These individuals fall under the dedicated employee dating persona. Their entire lives revolve around their job. When things are going good at work, they are happy. When the boss calls, they drop everything else to answer the phone. Their vacations consistently incorporate a part of their work responsibilities. The needs of their love interest rarely supersede the needs of the job. These individuals are loyal to their careers, and if they partake in dating, work will always have a seat at the table. Because of their loyalty to work, most people with these dating habits are very accomplished. They wouldn't give up so much of their lives for the sake of work if the rewards weren't great. For some, these rewards are financial, and for others, they are based on recognition and ownership. Small business owners will often fall in this category because of the time and effort required to sustain a small business. Many

Fortune 500 CEO's and CFO's also fit this persona because of the required personal sacrifices needed to obtain and sustain these types of positions. Dating someone like this typically requires an appreciation for great money management and job dedication. Though this isn't a guarantee, most people with this dating persona need their love interest to play the role of helpers. Their time is limited, and they don't want to be tasked with managing someone else's life. Therefore, being a burden to these individuals makes for some serious problems. This doesn't mean they won't try to spoil their love interest with expensive gifts and other pleasures. They just don't like to hear a lot of complaining. Once these career-driven individuals agree to long-term relationships, their significant others should expect to assist with protecting financial matters. This may not mean directly managing the money, but it will mean paying attention to all financial matters. Dedicated employee personas can't afford to stay with people who could potentially harm their reputation or hurt their chances of further career achievements. They need their partners to be an asset to their overall perception; therefore, being a good money manager or allowing someone else to ensure financial stability is a necessity. If you aren't willing to let someone else handle your money and have terrible money management skills, don't bother trying to create a long-term relationship with these individuals. You also shouldn't pursue a long-term relationship with people like this if you're unable to cope with a lot of money being used for the purpose of career advancement.

Don't be discouraged if you find that most people seem to fall under more than one dating personas. We are complex beings and limiting our behavior to one description is impossible. However, most people favor one dating persona more than the others. Whichever persona appears most frequently is the one you should trust in when they fit multiple personas. You should also think about how frequently you've dated people with the same or similar dating personas. If you find a trend, you may have identified the persona that attracts you the most. This new information will help you chose differently in the future. It can also reaffirm your self-perception, but don't be too overconfident or over critical. These dating personas are only a guide to understanding some likely financial habits of the people you are dating. They are a tool for evaluation during the infancy of a developing relationship. Once the relationship becomes a little more serious or discussions about creating a long-term relationship occur, you may become more comfortable with using this next tool to evaluate financial compatibility.

CREDIT REPORTS

Asking someone to exchange credit reports isn't easy. It has to be one of the most uncomfortable questions to ask someone who isn't your spouse or fiancé. This is why you shouldn't ask for one until the relationship has reached a point where marriage is being discussed. It's not normal for someone to ask for a copy of your credit report, and when people are asked to do something that isn't normal, they feel threatened and react based on those insecurities. These reactions can vary from mild annoyance to extreme aggravation, so it is imperative to be sure the relationship has reached a marital preparations stage. If you believe asking for a credit report won't potentially end the relationship, consider the nature of this request. In the United States, credit report requests are generally tied to nerve-wrecking job applications and the loan approval processes. Therefore, any request for a personal credit report makes people nervous. Think about your own life. When have you ever been asked for your credit report outside of these two situations? You probably haven't, and may feel threatened if it was asked for outside of these parameters. However, the unusual nature of this request shouldn't stop you from asking for one. If creditors use credit report to protect their assets, why shouldn't you? You're attempting to protect the most important assets in your life, your heart and time. Credit reports not only provide some of the most detailed personal financial information needed to assess financial stability, they also help to distinguish lies from truth. It's hard to fully convince someone of a lie when everything needed to disprove it is readily available, but simply obtaining a credit report copy isn't good enough. You also need to understand how to properly read a credit report.

Learning how to read credit reports is simple once you understand the basics. For starters, you need to be able to identify where each credit report is produced. The three major credit reporting agencies from which you can request a personal credit file from are Transunion, Experian, and Equifax. Each agency produces credit reports formatted based on their preferences, though all have some similarities. Here is a basic breakdown of the reporting format each agency utilizes:

Experian credit reports typically list the Inquiry data first, which includes some identifiers of who pulled the report, the consumer's name, social security number ("SSN"), the most up- to- date address on file, and keywords. Below this you will find the Report Header, Address, Employment History, Date of Birth, Aliases, Phone Number, Driver's License Number, and Fraud Summary (if applicable). Once you're through all the demographic information, a profile summary will appear. This provides a summary of total trade balances, past due totals, current derogatory trade items, and Old Trade Indicator, which will display the date of the oldest account on file. Next a FICO score and score factors will be listed, followed by all public records, which include liens, judgments, bankruptcy proceedings, child support rulings, etc. After all that information is listed, you will find actual trades; mortgage loans, auto loans, credit cards, collections accounts, etc. This is the main body of the credit report. Experian uses the following terms to describe trades:

SUBSCRIBER- The lender/creditor

SUB# - The lender's member number with Experian

Account Number

KOB – Kind of business code using letters A-Z to indicate what type of credit account is listed. The first letter is used to identify the primary classification, while other letters are secondary indicators. (Please check Experian website for most up to date coding.)

TYPE – Indicates the type of loan.

TERM – Indicates the length of an agreed upon loan term in months unless it is a revolving loan (REV).

ECOA – Indicates whether the responsibility for the account is individually, jointly, or partially owned.

OPEN – Date in which account was opened.

BALDATE and LAST PD – Dates of the balance being displayed and last payment.

AMT-TYP1 – An amount and a code identifying the amount.

BALANCE, MONTHLY PAY- The balance and monthly payment

AMT_TYP2 – A secondary amount and amount type.

PYMNT LEVEL – Date the account reached the current status

PAST DUE – Indicates the amount past due

ACCTCOND – Indicates whether account is open or closed

MOS REV – Number of months payment history on file

MAXIMUM – Date the worst status was reached

PYMT STATUS – Indicates if account current, delinquent, or in collections

After the body of the report you will find credit inquiries, creditor contact info and a space for consumer statements.

TransUnion (TU) credit reports read pretty similarly to the Experian credit report with slight, but important, differences. Of all the credit reports, I feel this one is the easiest to read because of its format. It begins with Inquiry Data, which includes TU Account Number, Consumer Name, SSN, Report Options, and Score Model Algorithm. After that you will see the Report Header, TransUnion Bureau Codes, Data Dates and Time, Infile Date, Alias, Current Address, Former Addresses, and Current and Former Employer Info. Next will be a Tran Alert, which indicates if there are any discrepancies on the report, followed by the Credit Summary. The Credit Summary lists everything in your credit report in groups such as delinquency history, estimated open balances and credit lines, mortgages, collection accounts, inquires, etc. After the summary you will find the Model Profile which shows the fico credit score and scoring factors. After the scoring section you will find a list of any public records and collections accounts. This section is important as it will reveal not only credit issues, but also judgments like child support and tax liens. The next section is the meat of the report - the Trade Lines, and this is where you will find the biggest differences between this report and the Experian report.

SUBNAME – Creditor

ACCOUNT NUMBER

ECOA - Indicates whether the account is an individual loan (1) or joint (2), or another like authorized user, co-applicant, etc.

INDUSTRY CODE - Kind of business code using letters A-Z to indicate what type of credit account is listed.

SUB# - Lender's subscription code with TU.

OPENED – Open date

VERIFIED – Date the account was last reported

CLSD/PD – Date acct was close or paid off

HIGH CRED – Highest balance

CREDIT LIMIT – Max amount of credit that can be used

BALANCE- Current balance

TERMS – Length of loan payoff period unless there is no term

PASTDUE – Amount past due

REMARKS

MAXDELQ – Date of worst delinquency

AMT_MOP – Amount and status code for worst delinquency.

MOP – Manner of payment status, current status of account

PAYMENT PATTERN – Up to twenty-four months of payment history (1= Up To Date, 2= thirty day, 3= sixty day, etc.)

After the trades you will find a list of Inquires, a Consumer Statement section, and Creditor Contact Info.

The Equifax credit report is also very reader friendly. It begins just like the other credit reports by listing consumer demographic information, a credit summary, a public records section, and potential fraud alerts. Once you get to the Trade Lines, you will begin to see what makes this report unique.

FIRM – Creditor

IDENT CODE – The lenders member Equifax member number

CS – Current Status (Revolving accounts start with an R, Installment loans begin with an I, and Open accounts that are less than 120 days past due begin with an O.)

ECOA – Code used to identify number of people responsible for debt. (Individual account (I), joint (C), Authorized User (A), Signer (M), etc.)

ACCOUNT NUMBER

RPTD, OPND – Last reported date and original account open date.

LIMIT – Credit limit

P/DUE – Current amount past due

HICR – Highest credit balance

TERM - Length of loan payoff period unless there is no term

BAL$ - Current balance

DLA – Date last reported

MR – Months reviewed

(30-60-90+) Number of thirty, sixty, and ninety - day delinquency marks

MAX – Dates and status code of worst delinquency

24 MONTH HISTORY – Up to twenty-four months of payment status codes (1= Up To Date, 2= thirty day, 3= sixty day, etc.) Reads left to right, with most current beginning on the left. After the trades you will find a list of Inquires, a Consumer Statement section, and Creditor Contact Info.

Be sure to always check for updates and reporting changes in the event that these reports are altered. If understanding these reports seems too difficult, don't worry about it. Most businesses that offer free credit reports and scores will provide their own version of a summary page, which is much easier to read. If given permission, try popular websites like freecreditreport.com or creditkarma.com for assistance. Remember, asking for a credit report creates discomfort, so make sure your relationship is on the brink of marriage first. If your special someone doesn't want to exchange report, don't get too bent out of shape. There are other factors that still need to be considered, and they can't be found on any credit report.

3

YOU, THE PARENT'S, AND THE CHILDREN

Before you commit to a long-term relationship with the parent of someone else's child or children, you need to fully understand the consequences of this choice. You are agreeing to form a relationship with a family. His or her children are going to want to be-friend you. Their ex will want to know about your background and character. You will lose more of your personal time due to having to convince others of your trustworthiness. Disputes centered on childcare and discipline will become a part of your weekly conversations, and your life will be totally altered. This is a big task for anyone to take on, but gaining a full grasp of this new environment will help you to adjust. Begin this process by examining the financial aspects of raising a child in today's economy.

Children are not cheap or expensive. They are a blessing to all families. Our lack of understanding the true cost of raising a child is what causes us to view children as expensive. How can a child be considered expensive when we make all decisions regarding their life? A child doesn't determine if he or she is born into a financially stable or unstable home. This is determined by the parents. Children don't decide where they will live or what school they will attend. They don't even decide if mommy and daddy will earn enough income to reasonable support the family. Children are bought into this world by their parents, and they determine if raising their child will be expensive. This is why it is important to understand the cost of raising a child before having one. Unfortunately many of us cannot go back in time and change some of the bad financial decisions we made. But it is never too late to prepare for the cost of raising children. Let's begin with the costs associated with infants.

Immediately after leaving the hospital, certain infant needs must be addressed. The newborn needs a place to sleep, all medicines prescribed by a physician, food, clothing, diapers, cleansers, traveling seat, and anything similar. They also need twenty-four hour supervision. These are only a few general descriptions of newborn needs. The costs associated with these needs will vary based on product market, location, family, and government assistance. Understanding these variations will better prepare parents to pay for them. Once a newborn has been home for a few months, many parents must transition some of their parental duties to a caretaker. Many employers offer their employees the opportunity to stay home with their newborns for a few months. Some will also distribute various levels of compensation. Once this time period expires, these parents will need to have someone assist with the caretaking of their child. This assistance is commonly filled by daycare providers, and the costs need to be considered. Parents should research potential daycare providers at least one year in advance. These services will likely be needed for the next three to four years.

As newborns become toddlers, their needs increase. All bedding, diapers, clothing, shoes, foods, traveling seats, and similar needs will have to be updated to account for their growth. These accommodations will be more expensive than before. Toddlers also need new toys and more complex games to satisfy their increased intelligence and curiosity. Number blocks and key rings are no longer sufficient. There are also other important changes taking place. During these years, children will gain playmates, and this will cause parents to occasionally accommodate for other toddlers. Adding a few dollars to the budget for other children is never a bad idea and should be practiced more frequently. Though children are going through many changes as toddlers, the next stage in their life presents more first-time expenses.

Preschoolers are very different from toddlers. They can communicate better and are more curious about the world around them. These children are at a stage where they need some form of education, and parents have some very important decisions to make. Almost all parents want their children to have the best opportunities to excel in life. To meet this desire, parents commonly enroll their toddlers into preschool or some similar learning center. This is where an important financial question must be answered. How much are we willing to pay for this medium? Some will pay as much as it takes to provide their children with the best education. Others will pay as much as they can reasonably afford. This choice will likely have a long-lasting effect, but not just for the children. This decision often determines the financial well-being of the entire household. It is difficult to provide the best education for children and settle for less than the best later in their lives. These schools that provide the best education have two things in common: high cost and loyalty. Parents that are willing to pay more for school do so because they don't want to send their children to underachieving schools. Once these parents become accustomed to expensive education costs fitting within their budget, it is never easy to change. This translates into being loyal to these types of schools.

Between the ages of five and nine, children will undergo rapid physical and mental advancements. Toddler clothes will quickly become too small and need to be replaced by more expensive clothes. Shoes will also need consistent replacement. But the largest jump in expenses will be related to social changes. During these years, children are more aware of the society around them and begin to develop their identity. They become involved in sports, music, afterschool programs, and many other extra-curricular activities. What do all these activities have in common? Most of them are not free. Parents need to be prepared for this financial change and adjust their budgets accordingly. This is also an age where children will want more expensive games and toys. Cries for dolls and cheap electronics will be replaced with calls for expensive video gaming systems. Peer pressure will drive them to consistently ask for the most popular clothes, toys, and gadgets. The house will frequently become boring and demand for vacations and family outings will increase. At this age, life is about the pursuit of fun, and parents have to bear the cost. This is another critical point where financial decisions must be made. How much money should parents spend to accommodate the wants of children? It was easier and cheaper to fulfill these wants when they were preschoolers. Most of their wants were inexpensive, and they weren't so aware of the world around them. Unfortunately, those times will never return, and how parents move forward will affect the household for years. Giving children whatever they want will likely cause financial problems and breed spoiled people. Not giving children enough can lead to resentment and cause them to look elsewhere for love. There is no perfect formula for all families to follow, but finding a happy medium is possible. Parents must always consider their financial well-being and commit to certain guidelines to be successful. Spending limits must be set, and childhood behavior in response to these limitations must be observed. If they fall out crying whenever they can't have something, their behavior needs to be addressed. They need to know their response to not getting something is unacceptable, unless you are okay with it. When they no longer share toys with others, maybe it's there needs to be a reduction in toy purchases. It is important to establish these types of boundaries while they are younger. Once children become pre-teens, it may be too late.

Preteens are children between the ages of ten and twelve. Based on their numerical age, this is a very short timeframe within childhood, but maturity levels may change at a faster pace. Some new expenses related to puberty will need to be addressed, but the biggest changes may be related to communication. By this time, children will probably want a cell phone, if they don't already have one. They want to be in constant contact with their friends, and the internet will not be enough. Many parents will also want their preteens to have a cell phone because of safety concerns. Preteens spend more time away from the home than ever before. Parents are well aware of how dangerous this world can be, and communication brings comfort. This combination of changes will result in higher expenses. While preteen years are short, the next stage in childhood will last much longer and require more money.

Teenagers require a lot of attention and create a need for more intricate financial planning. Their wants are more expensive. They cost more to feed. Education expenses reach an all-time high. But most importantly, they are transitioning into adulthood. Let's begin with examining the effect on household grocery expenses.

Teenagers eat a lot more than any other children in the household. They can eat as much as the parents and sometimes even more. Outside of food, there will also be an increased desire for toiletries and other cosmetic items. Expect at least a ten percent increase in grocery expenses. Clothes and shoes expenses will also see a sharp rise. This is a time when children have a stronger desire for self-identification. Their wardrobe is affected by this behavior. Teenagers frequently change their appearance, and their clothing is a lot more expensive than before. But, these changes are minor compared to the next set of new expenses. Most teens want to drive and adding a teenager to insurance plans is very costly. Parents should expect at least a one hundred percent increase in their insurance rates once they add a teenager to their policy. Driving school and drivers test fees also will need to be addressed. Parents who allow their teens to drive should also expect an increase in auto repair expenses. New drivers do not excel at keeping cars spotless. Buying teenagers their own car also comes at a high cost. The parents' car commanded a little more respect and couldn't be used as frequently. On the other hand, their car has more accessibility and doesn't require the same level of respect. This behavior is to be expected of a teen and so should an increase in expenses. Extra-curricular activity expenses will also rise. The cost of participating in class trips, field trips, school dances, proms, sports, school clubs, ring ceremonies, and similar activities will be higher than ever before. Somebody has to pay for the new football field and lab equipment. That burden belongs to the parents. Next up is the expense all parents should be prepared for: applying to and paying for post-high school graduation aspirations.

Before teenagers graduate from high school, their next step should already be addressed. This is something that can't be held off until the last minute. Parents have seventeen years to prepare for this moment, and those who didn't will have some tough decisions to make. This is not a decision that only parents of children who will go to college must decide. Parents with children that do not attend college or leave home also have an important decision to make. How much longer will they bear the living expenses of their child? Other parents must deal with their child transitioning to college. Application fees and campus visits should be the least of all concerns. The most important matter will be paying for college after the acceptance letters are received. Parents of children with full scholarships can relax during this process because this expense will be addressed or at least minimalized. Unfortunately, most parents won't have this luxury. These parents have an important decision to make. But, they shouldn't be too worried. This decision was made a long time ago, when the children were just preschoolers. Some parents decided to save for school and others didn't. Some decided to pay any price for education. Others choose affordable education options. The decisions made then will usually be the same decisions made now.

If you believe the relationship between your potential life partner and his or her child's father or mother should not and will not affect your relationship, you are in for a severe reality check. How much or how little this other parent is involved in the raising or his or her child will directly affect the dynamics of your relationship. When the other parent is not involved in the raising of his or her child, you are taking on the responsibilities of that absent parent. This also holds true when forming a relationship with someone that adopted their child or children. Your partner may not ask you to fill this role, but you can't love the mother or father without loving the child. If the other parent is a very active; you will need to understand how to play your role and not cause more harm than good. Don't be fooled into believing you won't have to develop some kind of relationship with the other parent because that's not realistic. No matter what type of parent your partners' ex-lover is, his or her behavior will affect your relationship, especially from a financial standpoint.

There are several ways to describe the financial habits of a single parent, but to better address the effect their behavior could have on your finances, I will use five categories to describe these parents.

Category 1: The Absent Parent

The absent parent is someone who has no financial relationship with his or her child. These individuals don't offer any type of financial assistance to the other parent for the purpose of raising their child. They don't make child support payments. They don't offer irregular or unscheduled financial assistance to help with the raising of their children. These absent parents are truly not concerned about the welfare of their children. Sometimes this behavior occurs because of a denial of parental responsibilities, or the other parent may not allow him or her to be involved in the parenting process. Whatever the reason, you need to understand that these parents will not be contributing. What does this mean for your finances? If you plan on forming a long-term relationship with the mother or father of this child, expect to include some expenses related to raising their child in your budgeting plans. Now, I 'm sure those of you in a relationship with a millionaire or wealthy person probably won't agree with me, but you are in the minority. Only a very small percentage of people in this country are in a relationship with someone like your partner. The rest of you should expect to contribute to these expenses on some level, and that requires good communication.

You must have a detailed conversation with your partner about your financial role, or lack thereof, in this relationship. Simply saying you will offer something to help out isn't good enough. It leaves too much open for personal interpretation. You need to be specific about your willingness to contribute. How much are you willing to help with education expenses? Are you going to purchase clothing, and how often? Will you help with the costs of extra-curricular activities? Having this conversation before taking your relationship any further will help to eliminate assumptions and unrealistic expectations. You don't want to jump into a situation where you're expected to offer assistance above your financial capabilities. Imagine the disappointment the child will have to experience. You should also consider the damage that will occur within your relationship when your partner's expectations are not met. Everyone loses when this occurs; therefore, you must be clear and concise about your planned financial contributions. You're not dealing with someone who can depend on the other parent. If you aren't up to this task, don't bother moving forward in this relationship. You will hurt too many people. Participating in this relationship will likely require you to be willing to offer some financial contributions. Many parents I've spoken to in this type of relationship have asked for significant contributions. Significant contributions means covering at least thirty-five to forty percent of the cost associated with raising a child. Setting these standards will help you to avoid unnecessary arguments, and it will strengthen your relationship.

Category 2: The Visitor Parent

Visitor parents limit their child raising financial contributions to an every thirty-five to ninety day time period. They are the true definition of a minimalist. If being sixty-one days past due on child support payments results in jail time, they will pay every sixty days. When money is needed for extra-curricular activities, they are nowhere to be found. Without a court judgment, these parents may let four months pass before sending some financial assistance. However, don't think about calling them a bad parent. They will battle you with everything they have to avoid this distinction. In their mind, being one step above a non-existent parent is sufficient and deserves a little praise. These individuals are a challenge to deal with peacefully, but you must endure this behavior if you plan on forming a solid relationship with their former partner and child. You are choosing to be in this relationship, and that means putting your feelings to the side for the sake of their child. Make room in your finances to compensate for the lapses of the visitor parent. Your partner may not ask you to fill these gaps, but you should attempt to do it anyway. It is better for you to attempt and be rejected, than to do nothing and appear disinterested. Besides, you're doing what's best for the child, not creating an excuse for the other parent to flee responsibility. Plan to cover at least twenty percent of all costs associated with raising their child unless asked not to, if you are sticking around for the long run. If this is a relationship that you don't plan on being in much longer, there is no need to make these adjustments. These are suggestions for those wanting to form a long-term bond.

Category 3: The Consistent Parent

Consistent parents are very involved in the upbringing of their children. They don't have full custody of their children, but try to visit or take them as much as possible. These are the parents that would love to have their children live with them, but are willing to accept the opposite. When their child needs help with homework or needs to be taken to baseball practice, they are up to the task. If they see a need for new shoes, clothes, books, or anything else, these items will be purchased. Consistent parents want the best for their children and refuse to miss a child support payment or not offer financial assistance when needed. While the relationship between this type of parent and your partner did not work out, they will not use it as an excuse to neglect their parental responsibilities. From a financial standpoint, these are the perfect type of parents to deal with while you're dating their former partners. You don't need to overcompensate for their behavior because it's unnecessary. Plan to help out with raising their child when needed, but don't overstep your boundaries. Consistent parents want to be certain their child knows they are helping, and you should try your best to not hinder their efforts. There will be many other issues that you have to address in this relationship, but they won't be related to finances. Just sit back and be available when needed.

Category 4: The Parent with Custody

All the previous categories represent a scenario where the person you are in a relationship has custody of all his or her children; however, this category represents the opposite. Jumping into this type of relationship presents an entirely different set of issues to consider. Some of these parents will try to take advantage of the other by asking for more money than the child needs. Others will try to eliminate the other parent's ability to participate in the raising of their child through the courts and legal system. There are also those who work well with the other parent and try to create the best possible relationship with their former lovers. Whatever the situation may be, it is your job to decide if you can endure this relationship. Staying in this relationship means accepting the financial demands of the other parent. Can you handle your partner being taken advantage of by their children's father or mother? While you may encourage your partner to limit their exposure to the former partners' greed, he or she may not agree with you. Your partner may feel it is acceptable for their ex-lover to take advantage of him or her. What will you do in this scenario? If you want to keep the peace, it is best to stay away from these matters. How about the moment you realize your partner doesn't offer enough financial to the child's other parent? Are you comfortable being in a relationship with someone who doesn't fully take care of his or her child? Is someone who isn't providing the financial necessities for his or her child trustworthy or financially capable of living with you? Are their issues long term or short term? While there are many reasons for someone not being able to support his or her child, acceptable reasons are far and few between. Do your best to answer these questions before the relationship becomes too serious. Otherwise, you will be setting yourself up for more stress in the future. Parents who don't provide financial support for their children risk imprisonment, wage garnishment, and often cause emotional damage to their children. How much of that are you willing to deal with? The responsibility of providing for a child doesn't disappear after a few years, so consider the circumstances before making a long-term commitment.

After considering all the factors that come with being in a relationship with a parent, are you prepared to adjust to this reality? If you've determined that you're not willing to adjust your time and budget to create a successful union with a parent, don't waste their time. Your reluctance should not make you feel guilty or shallow; it's just a reflection of your preferences. However, if you are ready for this type of relationship, don't allow anyone to convince you otherwise. While society has been more accepting of blended families and similar relationships, many still encourage others not to date people with children. You've already put thought into this potential relationship and should move forward with your decision.

4

PREPARING FOR THE COST OF A WEDDING

The decision has been made. You've asked the right questions and spoken with a counselor. You're comfortable with your partner's family and personal values. This is the person you want to spend the rest of your life with, and now it's time to think about ring shopping. How much should the budget be? What kind of ring will make both of you happy? The answers to these questions are very important. They will likely determine the financial stability of your future household.

Several years ago, I made one of the best decisions of my life by asking my steady girlfriend, Rachelle, to marry me. Before I could pop the big question, there was much work to be done. I had to begin the ring shopping and budgeting process. Being that I hated loans, I was determined to save enough money to purchase a ring. My job at the bank was paying me nearly $70,000 per year after bonuses were included, and my annual household expenses were limited to a little less than one third of my yearly income. This was pretty good for a guy that was only two years removed from graduating college with a bachelor's degree. Life was good. After taking my soon-to-be wife ring shopping, she narrowed her ring choices down to three. All were very similarly priced, and I could pay for them simply by saving two bonus checks and signing up for some overtime. Typically, I would've reached into my 401k savings for a loan to cover this expense, but my recent home purchase made that impossible. Once two month's passed, I saved enough money to purchase the engagement and wedding ring, and upgrade the engagement rings' diamond size by half a carat. I also made sure to insure the rings. Everything was perfect, but there was still some work to do. On the day in which I would ask Rachelle for her hand in marriage, I took her out to eat some crabs so that one of my friends could prepare the house for the proposal. I instructed him to use the roses I purchased to create a trail that led up to my office where a prerecorded video was setup with instructions that would eventually lead her to the place we met. She first had to play the video, go into the next room to open up a ring box with earrings and a note in it; (which was a joke,) and then go back to watching the video. After that, she was instructed to allow my friend, who was acting as a driver, to blind-fold her and take her to a secret destination. He was to drive her to the church where we met, sit her in the seat where I first saw her, and I would then remove the blind fold and offer my proposal. She began to cry as I kneeled down and professed my love for her, and instantly smiled when I presented her with an upgraded version of one of the rings she favored. Her reaction made all my efforts worth it. She happily said, "Yes."

One year later, we got married in front of about two hundred guests, and immediately flew to our honeymoon destination, Hawaii. Our life together was starting off great, but the beginning of a nationwide recession changed everything. The housing bubble burst, and as a result, my bank changed our pay structure. My income was reduced by nearly $30,000 dollars per year, and my wife was no longer working. This major setback eventually caused us to leave our home and downgrade our lifestyle, but not before putting up a great fight. We were able to come out of the recession with minimal damage, partially due to my early decision of not financing her wedding rings. I could have easily used my savings and a loan to purchase my wife a ring that was worth the price of some cars, but I didn't. A combination of sticking to my budget and having a girlfriend who didn't ask me to purchase a ring I really couldn't afford saved us from defaulting on a major loan. There would have been no way for me to pay back the money, and our marriage would have suffered because of it. Like most people in the United States, I had no idea one of the biggest recessions in history would occur. I was not prepared for such a huge drop in income within my household, even while living within my means.

Situations like this happen more often than expected, and it is important to consider them while making important financial decisions. While there may not be another recession for several decades, losing a job or experiencing a reduction in household income is not uncommon. When you're thinking about purchasing wedding rings, think about its long-term effect on the financial stability of your household. How much do you value having or giving a huge diamond ring versus being able to weather most financial storms? Celebrities and the media routinely encourage consumers to purchase the largest wedding rings possible, and to correlate ring size with love. At least ten to twenty engagement ring commercials are broadcasted each day, not counting repeats. It's almost impossible to go one day without seeing or hearing about some gigantic diamond engagement ring purchased for some celebrity. On top of all the media influence, you also have to deal with the expectation of your peers. What's the first thing most people want to see once they find out a woman is engaged? The ring her fiancé purchased. It's just an American norm, and it can be intimidating. Many people are terrified by the thought of someone looking at their ring and expressing any sort of disapproval or negative judgment, but you need to be more concerned with the financial stability of your marriage. The best way to protect this stability is to purchase these rings without the help of loans, but not everyone can do this. The next best option is to only obtain a loan that can be paid off within one to two years. This will limit the effect of most major household economic issues, like a twenty percent reduction in household income. Keeping your payment plans within these timeframes increase the likelihood of being able to maintain timely payments when major income reductions or expense increases occur. If your partner is not willing to accept either of these options, you need to seriously consider what this implies for the future. Don't believe that this will only happen once. If your future spouse would prefer you to risk the financial stability of your marriage on one upgradable purchase, don't expect his or her mindset to be different when it comes to other financial matters. The way a person goes about purchasing these rings is an early indication of how future financial decisions will be made. Once you've determined the ring shopping budget, it is time to prepare for the next step toward oneness, the wedding. And you better prepare for the costs.

The average cost of an American wedding is somewhere between $20,000 and $30,000. Some people choose to skip these costs by going to a local courthouse and getting married for a small fee, but most choose to partake in a more expensive ceremony. The reasons most people choose larger weddings can be traced back to their childhood desires and family traditions. Early in our lives we are constantly told our wedding day should be magical. This is the day most women have been looking forward to. Weddings fulfill a little girl's dream of being a princess for a day. It gives a young man the opportunity to watch his beautiful queen walk down the aisle to become his forever.

This is the stuff movies are made of and we are sold this dream for decades.

While it may be ideal for some of you to find that special someone with a desire for a cheap and inexpensive wedding, don't get your hopes up. Most of us are destined to marry someone that will at least want an average American wedding. Here's a list of some expenses you should expect to encounter as you plan your wedding: ceremony location, ceremony officiator, ceremony decorations, flowers, limo rental, wedding planner, wedding dress, veil, tuxedo, suit, musicians/soloist, photographer, videographer, programs, gifts and favors, invitations, guestbook, thank you cards, beauty and spa services, wedding rings, reception location, reception food services, reception bar services, reception decorations, wedding cake and dessert

With so many expenses to consider before honeymoon costs are added, creating a plan to cover these costs should be a major priority. Don't fool yourself into believing this process is a short-term dilemma. If these expenses are not taken care of correctly, the wedding can be the spark that destroys your marriage. Imagine not being able to fully pursue your career ambitions because of a negative credit report. How would you feel if your children couldn't attend the best schools because of a loan that was taken to finance your wedding? What about not being able to take a vacation each year or not being able to leave an undesirable neighborhood? Wedding-related debts can linger over a newly formed family for years and prevent lifestyle-goal achievement. You don't want to endure the stress that comes with trying to build a family while paying off a lot of debt. It will ultimately cause your marriage to suffer. Preparing for the cost of this epic event is a necessity, so begin this process by having a conversation with the parents.   Are your future in-laws prepared to contribute towards wedding expenses? How about your parents? Do they believe their financial responsibilities to this wedding should follow American traditions or the traditions of another nation? Don't make the mistake of assuming people will act according to your own expectations. Some parent's don't expect to pay for rehearsal dinners and reception locations. It is you and your spouse's job to have a clear and concise conversation with your family to ensure everyone understands their financial responsibilities related to the wedding. Here are a few questions that will help you to accomplish this task: ceremony location, ceremony officiator, ceremony decorations, flowers, limo rental, wedding planner, wedding dress, veil, tuxedo, suit, musicians/soloist, photographer, /videographer, programs, gifts and favors, invitations, guestbook, thank you cards, beauty and spa services, wedding rings, reception location, reception food services, reception bar services, reception decorations, wedding cake and /dessert

With so many expenses to consider before honeymoon costs are added, creating a plan to cover these costs should be a major priority. Don't fool yourself into believing this process is a short-term dilemma. If these expenses are not taken care of correctly, the wedding can be the spark that destroys your marriage. Imagine not being able to fully pursue your career ambitions because of a negative credit report. How would you feel if your children couldn't attend the best schools because of a loan that was taken to finance your wedding? What about not being able to take a vacation each year or not being able to leave an undesirable neighborhood? Wedding-related debts can linger over a newly formed family for years and prevent lifestyle-goal achievement. You don't want to endure the stress that comes with trying to build a family while paying off a lot of debt. It will ultimately cause your marriage to suffer. Preparing for the cost of this epic event is a necessity, so begin this process by having a conversation with the parents.

Are your future in-laws prepared to contribute towards wedding expenses? How about your parents? Do they believe their financial responsibilities to this wedding should follow American traditions or the traditions of another nation? Don't make the mistake of assuming people will act according to your own expectations. Some parent's don't expect to pay for rehearsal dinners and reception locations. It is you and your spouse's job to have a clear and concise conversation with your family to ensure everyone understands their financial responsibilities related to the wedding. Here are a few questions that will help you to accomplish this task:

- What, if any, wedding expenses are you prepared to pay?
- What expectations do you have for this wedding?
- Are you aware of the traditional financial expectations of the parents of the bride and groom? Do you care about them, or are they irrelevant to you?
- Have you saved any money to use for this wedding?
- Have you spoken with the bride or groom's parents about how much they are willing to contribute to this wedding?

Once these issues are covered, you can begin to plan your financial contributions, if necessary.

How much of your future income are you willing to commit to the cost of your wedding? Couples with money set aside for wedding expenses don't have to worry about this question, but everyone else should have an answer before walking down the aisle. Using a bank loan is the most popular way to fund weddings in the absence of savings, but they come with a big cost. You can expect to pay anywhere from one to sixteen percent interest on these personal loans, and default penalties can increase these rates. You also need to consider any potential late fees, annual fees, and other miscellaneous fees linked to all loans. We never plan to make a late payment on any loan, but unexpected expenses always occur, and the penalties must be factor into decision making. Before agreeing to finance your wedding with loans, I suggest you to account for the potential total cost of each loan and compare it to your current earnings. Use the formulas below to assist you with these calculations.

Formula 1

Take the total cost of loan or loans with no late payments (use loan term as estimated payoff date or five years) /and divide it by the total earnings (use loan term or five years to estimate accumulated earnings).

Example: I can reasonably expect to earn $250,000 in gross income over the next five years, and this loan will reach a total cost of $25,000 over five years. (If you need assistance with estimating the total cost of your loan, use an online loan estimator calculator on sites like MoneyEtiquette.com)

$$\$25,000 / \$250,000 = .1 \text{ or } 10\%$$

Therefore; agreeing to this loan equates to giving up ten percent of my potential gross income over the next five years.

Formula 2

Total cost of loan or loans with default penalty rate (use loan term as estimated payoff date or five years) / Total earnings (use loan term or five years to estimated accumulated earnings)

Example: I expect to earn $250,000 in gross income over the next five years and this loan will reach a total cost of $30,000 over five years based on the default rate.

$$\$30,000 \,/\, \$250,000 = .12 \text{ or } 12\%$$

Therefore, agreeing to this loan and defaulting on the payments will result in losing twelve percent of my potential gross income. (You can substitute gross income with net income if that's a preference.)

When you begin to evaluate your results be sure to consider the following facts:

Most mortgage payments typically account for twenty to twenty-eight percent of gross income.

Income taxes, social security, and medical benefits typically account for twenty-five-to-thirty-three percent of gross income.

Auto loan payments typically account for one to five percent of gross income.

While these equations may provide great financial data to help you with wedding-related spending decisions; emotional factors should also be considered. You and your soon-to-be spouse need to really understand how much this wedding means to each other. If you've always dreamed of having a big wedding, be honest about your feelings. If your heart is set on having a destination wedding, express that desire. The worst thing you can do in this situation is remain silent for the sake of peace and happiness. You must communicate your expectations to give your future spouse a real opportunity to respond to them. If he or she isn't comfortable with your desires, it is better for this to be known than hidden. Don't allow fear to keep this conversation from happening. You are marrying this person, and wedding expectations should never be used as an excuse to cancel a wedding. If your fiancé uses this as a way to escape the marriage, he or she didn't really want to get married in the first place, and it's better to know this before the wedding date. Make sure all wedding desires have been discussed and determine what options are affordable based on your prior research. It is likely that not all desires will be met, but a compromise can be found. Remember, what you can't afford to do today can be accomplished in the future. This may mean having small wedding, but a big ten or twenty-year anniversary celebration. It could also mean delaying having children or moving into a large house. Whatever you both decide to do, make sure all these issues are addressed. If you don't, resentment will build up and can surface in other household matters.

5

WHEN TWO BECOME ONE

The wedding is over. Vows have been exchanged. You've returned from the honeymoon, and you're ready to truly begin the next chapter in your life called marriage. Your family, friends, counselors, and others have offered loads of advice about how to transition into this new chapter in your life with ease, but now it's time to put theories into action. Now you have to do something that requires patience, humility, strength, courage, honesty, and everything else that defines love. You actually have to build a life with someone who was raised in a different home. This person didn't learn the same household habits you learned as a child. He or she didn't see your father pay all the bills while your mother stayed home to raise you. There were no cooking lessons or household chores where they grew up. He or she has never seen a real marriage or never had parents that lived together. This person was raised without siblings and never spent much time with other family members. Whatever the case may be, there is one undeniable truth about getting married: you are truly dealing with someone who is somewhat foreign to your world, and it is your job to create a lifelong relationship with him or her. With such a daunting task in front of you, it is understandable to feel insecure about your future. It is reasonable to feel the need to flee this responsibility or to not make mistakes that could potentially ruin this relationship. This is a totally new experience for you and there is much to learn, but you must embrace this difficult challenge for your marriage to have a great chance of succeeding. My marriage wouldn't be where it is today, had I not embraced this reality.

When Rachelle and I were dating, we both walked into the marriage with some bad expectations. Sure, we both came from households with a mother and father, were born and raised in Baltimore City, and attended the same church, but even those commonalities didn't exempt us from having to endure the challenge of creating a unified household. Rachelle came from a household that was a little more free flowing than my own. Her dad was the authority figure within the household, but wasn't very strict. Her mother was a fun-loving but stern jokester who sacrificed personal ambitions for the sake of her children. And her younger siblings were sarcastic comedians who followed her lead. They also had a fun-loving dog named Lucky, and lived in what most people outside of the city would call a dangerous neighborhood. The rest of us just view it as another block in B-more. Their house, a typical Baltimore row home, was near the beginning of the street, and was known to be a welcoming place. Family members, neighborhood kids, and church members frequently passed through their home to share meals, stories, and a few good laughs. It was quite a nice home to grow up in, but there was one drawback. They only had one bathroom to share amongst five and sometimes six or seven people, which forced everyone to become a little less shy if they weren't already.

My household, on the other hand, was a bit different. My father was a strict, hard-working recovering alcoholic. My mother was a straight-forward woman who had little tolerance for nonsense. My older sister was a bossy, but lovable, sibling who sometimes broke the household rules. Like my in-laws, we lived in a row home for about nine years and then moved to a single-family home on the same side of the city. When we lived in the row home, the household didn't attend church, but that changed once we moved. My father stopped drinking, turned his life over to Christ, and demanded our household to become more conservative. Most of Rachelle's family had been raised in the church, but serving God wasn't always the focus of my household until we moved. The feel of my new home was more like a machine than the old one. My parents were all about operating as one efficient unit. Everyone had a job to do, and once we became of age, we were expected to earn some money. I can even recall my mother telling me that I was cute, but broke, and needing to work when I was in middle school. If you weren't making money in my house, you were going to be ridiculed, but with love. These differences and many more stayed with us as we began to build our household, and led to many arguments. I thought Rachelle should see things my way, and she felt the opposite. She was focused on creating an easy-going and love-filled household, while I was more focused on efficiency. Ultimately, we both had to learn to put our differences aside and create our own household, instead of bringing the ones we were raised in with us. This is something we still battle with today, but have learned to overcome these issues. Yes, we grew up in similar settings and circumstances, but we were and still are two different people trying to become one.

Despite the gravity of this challenge, I do have some good news to share with you. There is one person you will always be able to control in this relationship: yourself. Though you are working towards oneness with your mate, you will always have the ability to control one half of this union. You control how much effort you will put into creating a lasting marriage. Your spouse can't force you to do anything that you don't want to do, but the bad news also resides within this truth. Unfortunately, you have no control over the decisions your spouse will make. All the hard work and love you bring into the relationship will not guarantee duplication from your spouse. It is totally his or her choice to make the necessary sacrifices for the sake of the marriage. Therefore, you need to ask yourself if you're willing to be open to this level of vulnerability. That is what makes a marriage so special. Each person must be willing to be vulnerable to the other for the marriage to work, but that doesn't mean you have to be a fool. While most people believe being vulnerable and being fooled are always intertwined, they are not. You can be vulnerable without being a fool to another person's trickery, especially when it comes to finances.

How is it possible to be totally vulnerable with your spouse and not be open to the possibility of being turned into a fool? The answer is quite simple. Anticipation and accurate perception diminishes the probability of feeling foolish. If you learn the financial habits of your spouse, you will be better prepared to handle the repercussions of the financial decisions that make you feel uncomfortable. We spend decades in school to prepare for our future careers. Why shouldn't we be just as diligent when preparing to become one with our spouse? Remember, you vowed to be with this person until death. That means you have a lot of time to study your mate even if you didn't do a lot of research before getting married, but avoid procrastination. Taking your precious time studying your spouse increases the chances of feeling foolish, so make this one of your top priorities as you build your marriage.

There are several steps you can take to better learn the financial habits of your spouse. The first step is the most obvious one: have a productive conversation with him or her about financial matters. Healthy communication with your spouse will lead to fewer misunderstandings, and you need to understand how to create these conversations. To do this successfully, you need to learn your partner's language. While both of you may speak English or another language, there is a high probability that you don't define all words in the same manner. In your partner's mind, the word few, when used in the context of time, may mean exactly three minutes, while it may be defined as five minutes in your mind. Responsible budgeting could mean creating a document which tracks all financial transactions from your perspective, but it might be interpreted as simply being aware of all checking and savings accounts balances to your spouse. These differences are often seen as problems, but they are actually the solution to most marital disputes. If you know your spouse defines a few minutes as three minutes, accept his or her interpretation. When your spouse defines budgeting as simply knowing the balances in all checking and savings accounts, you need to hear it that way. Far too often, people reject words and phrases used by others simply because they see it as a threat to their own interpretations, but thinking this way creates more problems. Their different use of the English language won't weaken your method of conveying messages. It is possible to be content with these differences, but doing this takes practice. You can begin by writing down the most common phrases your spouse uses that irritates you. As you review this list, divide these phrases into quarters and practice being receptive to their use. Do this for the next thirty days and move on to the next quarter of your list. By doing this, you are teaching yourself to not feel threatened by these phrases. Once you've finished this task, attempt to have a conversation about finances with your spouse. Ask him or her as many open-ended questions as possible. Closed questions can cause people to feel attacked, so avoid these to get the most informative responses. If you don't know where to start, here are a few questions you may want to use:

- How would you like our household to be structured from a financial perspective?
- What don't you like about my financial habits?
- What financial decisions do you believe we should make together?
- What financial habits are you absolutely opposed to?
- What are your lifestyle goals?

Another step that can be taken to help you understand the financial habits of your spouse is to track his or her spending habits. While this task may have been difficult when you were dating, it is much easier to perform when you're married. It doesn't matter if you do or don't have a joint checking account; there are still plenty of ways to track your spouse's spending. The first thing you can do is look around your home for clues. When you look in the closet, are his or her clothes primarily from one or two designers? How many pairs of shoes do your spouse own and how old are they? Do you see any unopened or past-due bills lying around? Is your caller ID filled with missed calls from bill collectors? I could go on and on about this, but I'm sure you get the point by now. Remember, this is not a search for bad news or things that will help you to criticize your spouse. You are simply gathering clues to gain better insight to his or her financial decisions. Once you're done looking inside the house, make sure you note any habits you've been able to identify, and look for new clues outside your home.

Possessions like cars, boats, bikes, and other vehicles can tell you a lot about your partner's financial habits. How often does your spouse like to upgrade vehicles? Is pay the primary motivator behind your spouse's automobile purchasing choices? If not, what is his or her primary motivator? Are all his or her vehicles used primarily for transportation to work? You need to know the answers to these questions and more if you're really interested in knowing your spouse's financial habits. The decision-making process that leads to these purchases is typically tied to lifestyle goals and public perception ideals. Many people base their vehicle purchasing decisions on social norms. In the United States, the average doctor, lawyer, professional athlete, investment banker, CEO, Billboard Top 100 artist, and other socialites are expected to own or drive luxury class or high performance vehicles. Those that do not are considered strange or unusual. At the same time, teachers, janitors, secretaries, customer service representatives and entry-level workers are expected to drive more modest vehicles. The desire to be perceived as a person that accepts these norms affects all purchasing decisions, and evaluating vehicle purchases can assist with evaluating the strength of this desire.

If the previous steps don't work, it is time to reach out for help. Yes, now is the moment you need to seek out family members for assistance. Close family members like parents or siblings often provide great insight about the financial habits of significant others. They were there while your spouse developed his or her financial habits. From the first time your spouse learned about money until he or she moved out, these people were going along for the ride. Use their memories and advice to help you along this journey of understanding, but also be very careful. Being overzealous could result in more problems and create unneeded tension between you and your spouse. To prevent this from occurring, you need to follow these few rules:

Do not approach family members with a negative disposition.

Negativity breeds concern, and these family members will reach out to your spouse if you create a sense of trouble. When you speak to these family members, do so with a humble tone. Let yourself be the one that appears to need help, rather than your spouse. You can do this by explaining how the information being sought will help you become a better spouse. This isn't an attempt to gather backers for the sake of winning an argument; you want to know your spouse better, and they have the information you need.

Pay attention to childhood stories about your spouse and keep mental notes about all financial matters.

These are the moments that you don't have to ask anything about your spouse, and still get the information you need. When visiting family members, always ask to see some family photos and the stories will come in bunches.

Ask your mother- and father-in-law about their marriage, divorce, or relationship.

The financial habits your spouse has developed can usually be tied to one or both of his or her parents. Ask questions about where they lived and what type of jobs they had or have. The answers will help you to understand what type of financial household your spouse was raised in.

Stay away from your spouse's closest friends.

Close friends are also not always the best source for information about your spouse's financial habits. While close friends will typically know a lot about your spouse, they may not be aware of what really goes on with your spouse's financial matters.

Use everything you've learned from all your research to identify your partners money personality.

Use the same personalities from "IT ALL BEGINS WITH YOU", (chaser, builder, manager, and victim) and chose the personality or personalities that best fit your spouse. This will be easier if your spouse elects to self-identify, but base your choice on your research if he or she did not. After identifying your spouse's money personality, you need to figure out what your type of financial structure your partner prefers for your household.

Family members can offer more than insight about your spouse; their customs will also help you to better your partner. We all have very complex relationships with our family members, and they affect every marriage. Some people keep their personal matters away from family members and others don't. These differences are often based on the financial structure of each household. There are four financial structures most families fall under: intra-household, multi-household, generational, and total inclusion.

Intra-household families share financial gains and losses exclusively with household members. These families do not consider people outside of their household in financial decision making. Outside family members may receive gifts, but there is no regard for their financial well-being. Spouses from this family structure usually bring minimal family expenses to the marriage. When family members outside of the home need financial assistance, they will not attempt to assistance.

Multi-household families share their financial gains and losses with some family members. They consider some family members in their financial decision making, but will purposely exclude others. This behavior occurs for several reasons. The most frequent cause is a strained relationship. Changes in these relationships also move family members in and out of this structure. Some family members may remain a consistent part of financial planning, while other may not. Uncle Jeff may be considered this month and not considered in the future. These families must consistently discuss family financial issues because of frequent changes. They have a wide range of expenses to discuss and it is important to be prepared.

Generational families share financial gains and losses based on generation. This is usually determined by average age between mother and child. There is a consistent vertical movement of assets and debts. Adult siblings will not consider each other in financial decisions, but do include their children, nieces, and nephews. Parents look to their children for assistance as they grow older. The next generation is always the focus and estates are often left in their care. People from this family structure bring consistent family expenses to their marriage. They can calculate how much their family members will affect the household income more easily than others. The reason is because there are a set number of family members to consider. The dynamics of multi-household families consistently change, but generational families are more stable. They only change financial plans based on births and deaths.

Unlike the generational model, total inclusive families share financial gains and losses with all family members. Bloodline is the usual method of determining membership, and this practice is commonly found within royal families. Their goal is to ensure all family members are financially stable. They do this to maintain some level of high social status or guarantee a long-lasting lineage. Spouses in this family usually bring expenses based on family wealth. If they come from poor families, expenses will be very high. If they come from wealthy families, family expenses will usually be lower. Marriages fail and succeed based on the understanding of these financial structures. When couples understand their money personality and structure, they are better fit for future financial challenges.

Now that you've gained a better understanding of your spouse's financial habits, and have a good grasp of your financial mindset, it is decision-making time. Before you begin to create a financial plan with your spouse, you need to decide how much or what you are willing to part with for the sake of creating a financially compatible household. This is a difficult task, but it must be done to avoid future conflicts. By making these decisions before discussing finances with your partner, you are agreeing to sacrifice something you hold dear before anger makes this task impossible to complete. In the heat of the moment, people are rarely able to compromise even when they know they are wrong. Take this time to really come up with an idea of what you are willing to lose. While you may not be able to feel totally confident in your ability to part with these things or comfort, you need to at least attempt this exercise. People can never be totally sure of how they'll react to situations they've never experienced, but it doesn't hurt to mentally prepare for these moments.

Once you've prepared your mind for possible financial and mental comfort losses, it is time to sit down with your spouse and create a tangible plan. This process should begin with planning a "dreams and aspirations date night." Talking about financial matters in the home can be uncomfortable and cause tension because of certain emotional ties to the home. The early stages of mutual financial planning should take place in a location that promotes neutrality and compromise. Try planning an evening visit to a restaurant that neither of you are familiar with. This place should be quiet enough to hold a conversation, but not so fancy that you will have to neglect household bills to eat an entire meal. During this date, don't bring anything to take notes. The conversation about your financial plans should be limited to overall lifestyle goals. This is an opportunity for you to listen and share your aspirations without consequence or criticism. The goal of this conversation is to create the end goals which will drive most of your mutual financial plans. When this task has been completed, feel free to chat about anything else, but do not talk about any other financial matters. It is important to not ruin your great strides by stepping into another conversation that could derail your progression.

The next step to creating a tangible financial plan is to set aside some time for you and your spouse to determine how you will move forward. It should not be assumed that because you were able to survive the previously mentioned date night, you are ready to sit down and create a financial plan with your spouse. Now is the time to determine if it is possible for you to create a financial plan without outside assistance. If your money personalities, ideal financial household structure, and overall lifestyle goals are polar opposites, you are more than likely in need of third-party help. This assistance can come in the form of a spiritual counselor, financial adviser, marriage counselor, or a great book. Those that are more aligned with each other from a financial perspective should at least attempt to move forward with creating a financial plan.

Creating your first financial plan as a couple should get a bit easier from this point going forward. You've already done the hard work with the previous exercises, so it is time to get down to the numbers. Begin this process by estimating the cost of obtaining your compatible lifestyle dreams. These are the aspirations that are able to coincide or co-exist if obtained. For example, you can't expect to live in a Mexico and Paris at the same time, but you can purchase rental properties in both locations. Use resources like Zillow.com, Bankrate.com, CNN Money, and Jumpstart.org to assist you with estimating these costs. You can also consult real estate brokers and retirement experts for assistance. Once you've obtain your estimates, it is time to come up with the timeframe in which both of you would like to obtain these lifestyle goals. Do you want to reach this goal within the next ten years or thirty years? The combination of your mutual lifestyle goal costs estimates and timeframe goals comprise the foundation of your financial plan. Now that you've created the framework of your plan, it is time to estimate the feasibility of your goal achievement plans.

Determining feasibility requires a complete understanding of your monthly income and expenses, and your total assets and total liabilities. You need to be able to understand how much money you can save based on your current living expenses, and how close you are to paying off your long-term debts. To accurately assess your monthly income and expenses, you need to account for real income and all monthly expenses you should be paying. Real income is money you are either guaranteed to earn or likely to earn without the need of abnormal financial gains. Occasional bonuses, possible raises, and other skeptical funds should not be counted as real income. Including these potential earnings could put your entire plan in jeopardy. You should also be sure to only use net monthly income to ensure accuracy. Once you've accounted for everything, subtract your total monthly expenses from your total monthly net income. What you are left with will determine your next move.

If your total monthly expenses are greater or equal to your total monthly net income, it is time to make some serious changes. You aren't financially stable, and never will be at this pace. You may want to consider moving into a less costly home, discontinuing the use of unnecessary services (gym memberships, online video memberships, cable or satellite service, etc.), and eliminating any other luxury expenses. If you can't make these changes because you don't have the will power to do so, consider contacting a non-profit credit counseling service provider. The outcome of this call will likely lead you to either consolidating your debt, filing bankruptcy, or just reorganizing your bill payment strategy. If you are too embarrassed about your finances to request third-party assistance, here are a few tips that may help you with eliminating debt and increasing your cash flow:

Prioritize your monthly expenses based on need before attempting any aggressive bill pay down plan. Monthly expenses related to shelter, food, clothing, home energy, communication, religious obligations, child care, spousal care, parental care, non-college education costs, transportation, and medical coverage's should be at the top of this list. Personal loans that are still with the original lender (not charged off) and not attached to any property (credit cards, student loans, personal loans, medical loans) should be secondary. All other outstanding monthly expenses can be listed after those previously mentioned.

If the top priorities listed above cannot be covered by your current monthly income, you must make some serious lifestyle changes. This may result in moving to less expensive dwellings, which may include living with family members. Other drastic changes that may be needed include: voluntary auto repossession, elimination of unnecessary cell phone plans, and applying for public assistance.

If the first two steps are not possible, consider contacting a bankruptcy attorney. This method of debt elimination should only be used when you have no other choices. If you are unable to move out of your home or eliminate or reduce your secured loan payments, this may be your only choice.

If you are only able to pay your first and second-level monthly expenses, pay down monthly bills that will increase your cash flow before attacking your non-essential debts. Debts that can be paid off the fastest should be paid first. These are debts with low balances and high payments. Loans with identical balances should be prioritized based on monthly payments; the highest payment should be paid off first. This type of payoff plan requires aggressive payments. Paying five dollars above the minimum payment is not aggressive. Payments need to be increased by at least twenty-five percent. If this isn't possible, it is ok to add less.

If you fall into the group where your total monthly net income, which is your take home pay, exceeds your total monthly expenses, the feasibility of your goal achievement plans will be based on the rate in which you are able to increase your net-worth. The speed in which you increase this total will determine how quickly you achieve your mutual lifestyle goals. That is why increasing your total net -worth is so important. Though it is possible to pay monthly bills without being late while having a negative total household net -worth, it certainly won't help with achieving your lifestyle goals. Make sure your financial plans include at least a one percent annual increase in net -worth, even if you're starting off in the red; having a negative net-worth. Remember, your net-worth is calculated by subtracting your total liabilities from your total assets, and if you're starting out with negative total net-worth, your focus should be on getting back to even. For all those with positive total household net -worth, here are a few steps you can follow to help assess the feasibility of your lifestyle goals:

Do your research. Use the advice of real estate experts, asset appraisers, travel agents, financial advisers, and anyone else that can provide an accurate cost estimate of your lifestyle goals. You can also use websites like Zillow.com and BankRate.com for helpful information.

Compare your current total household net -worth with the estimates you've obtained from the previous step.

Example: If your household's net-worth was $39,000 in 2012, and it was $37,000 in 2011, then you had a $2,000 net-worth increase. If for 2013 your net-worth increased to $41,000, you've maintained a $2,000 net-worth increase for a two year period.

*Using at least two years of data will help to account for annual anomalies, but feel free to use more.

In this example, your household has experienced a $2,000 increase in net-worth for the last two years. Base on this example, if your household has a current net-worth of $41,000 and needs at least $120,000 to reach your lifestyle goals, how much more money do you need to reach this goals? The answer is $79,000. Based on your current rate of total annual net-worth increase, $2,000 per year, it will take you approximately thirty-nine years to be able to afford the cost of your lifestyle goals. Keep in mind, while you could use loans to reach this figure more quickly, the costs of such loans and its impact to your current total net-worth must be considered. Use the formulas in this example to figure out the feasibility of your lifestyle goals. If you find that you won't be able to achieve these goals before your seventieth birthday, it is probably best to revise these goals. Unfortunately, you are not likely to achieve these goals without major asset increases or liability decreases. That doesn't mean you should stop trying, but you may need to create more realistic goals.

Revising your mutual lifestyle goals will not be an easy task. Either one or both of you will have to make some changes for the purpose of creating a mutually beneficial financial plan, and that's never easy. Begin by revisiting the losses you agreed to endure for the sake of unifying your household. If you've skipped over the part of the book that addresses these losses, go back a few paragraphs before reading on; otherwise, move forward. How do these losses affect your financial plans? Do they alter your overall lifestyle goals enough to increase the likelihood of goal achievement? If they do, use them to revise your mutual lifestyle goals. If the losses do not increase the feasibility of reaching your lifestyle goals, you both need to make some changes. This is the hard part. It is likely that neither you nor your partner wants to sacrifice more lifestyle ambitions for the sake of this union, but it has to be done. Ignoring this problem often leads to divorce or unhappy marriages, and it is best to resolve this issue now, if possible. Take some time to yourself and re-evaluate your lifestyle goals. Think about what you need least within your goals and try to alter them based on the cost analysis you performed earlier. Remember, the purpose of making these changes is to increase the feasibility of your mutual plans. It is still possible for you to obtain these lifestyle goals, but they must be altered for the purpose of financial planning and creating compatibility. Once you've made some alterations, prepare to go back to your spouse and talk about them. Don't be overzealous and plan on having this conversation minutes after you couldn't come to an agreement. Make sure you give yourself a few days to minimize any tensions that may have arisen from your last conversation. You will know the right time to approach your spouse. When the time comes to continue this conversation, share your revised goals with your spouse and figure out if enough has changed for you to move forward. If you aren't there, go through the revision process again until your mutual goals become feasible.

Now that your mutual lifestyle goals are realistic and possible to reach before the age of seventy, create a one year plan that aligns with them. For example, if you need to average a $5,000 annual increase in total household net-worth, make room for at least a $417.00 monthly reduction in liabilities or a $417.00 increase in savings and asset growth. Revisit your list of total monthly income and total monthly expenses, and try to make adjustments to incorporate the changes needed to achieve your mutual lifestyle goals. Your feasibility test has already proven that it is possible for you to reach your goals, but you still need to implement a plan that will get you there. Doing this successfully will help you create a financially unified household, but if you aren't able to get past major disagreements with your partner, don't give up. It may still be possible to resolve these issues, but it's going to take some hard work.

6

CONFLICT RESOLUTION

What happens when two people come together and attempt to create a unified lifetime partnership? Conflict or disagreements will arise. There is no way to avoid it. No two people will ever agree on everything, especially when it comes to financial matters. Budgeting, banking, spending, money handling, saving, and all other financial habits will be debated within a marriage, and the outcome of these arguments can often determine its fate. Those who are able to overcome differences are more likely to remain married, while others usually head towards divorce. The key to being a part of the group that overcomes these problems resides in the ability to effectively communicate and adjust for the sake of the relationship. Couples that learn to overcome their language barriers and are willing to work through different financial philosophies have the tools needed to resolve most financial based conflicts.

I remember when my wife and I had our first financial disagreement. We had only been married for a few months and were attempting to decide how we would handle our bank accounts. I was in favor of having several joint accounts, while my wife wanted to have at least one separate account. Her request sparked some uncomfortable feelings. I instantly believed she didn't trust me with all her money and felt a little betrayed. If she couldn't trust someone in the banking field to handle financial affairs, who could she trust? Well, at least that was the question racing through my mind. I'd also come up with what I thought was the only reasonable cause of her behavior: trust issues. This was totally the wrong approach to this situation. Before considering her actual reasons for wanting her own checking account, I created my own reasons. We went back and forth about this issue for a few weeks until I ultimately gave in to her desires. I figured if she was happy, we'd both be happy, but nice sayings don't often address real problems. Though Rachelle had her own personal issues that caused her to take the stance she took, I simply chose to ignore them and give in for the sake of a peaceful home. I had a listening and consideration problem that needed attention, and was fortunate enough to have people in my life to get me on the right track. My mentors helped me to understand what works in marriage. They taught me to deal with my own issues and put more importance on understanding versus assuming. Rachelle and I eventually spoke about her reasons for wanting her own checking account. Her reasons had nothing to do with a personal distrust for me. She didn't mind me having full access to her account or managing our money. All she wanted was to establish a few accounts in her name and build her credit. This entire situation could have been avoided if I'd been a better communicator, and more humble. I was inexperienced with conflict resolution, and began at the wrong place.

Conflict resolution begins with self and peer -evaluation. Before you start criticizing your spouse, be critical of yourself. Begin by examining the manner in which you communicate with others. Write or type a self-evaluation of your communication skills using the following categories: speaking-to-listening ratio, vocabulary and use of slang, body language, frustration limits, and tone. Under each category, describe how you view yourself. Are you more of a talker or listener when conversing? What kind of vocabulary do you use in non-professional environments, and do you use a lot of slang? What kind of body language do you use during a conversation? How easily do you get frustrated when speaking with others? What is your normal speaking tone? Be honest with yourself and evaluate yourself to the best of your abilities. Next, ask some of your family members and close friends to describe your communication style and skills. Use the same categories and questions used for your self-evaluation for this step. If the people you have in mind for this task are not brave enough to be completely honest with you, move on. You need people that are not afraid to hurt your feelings. Below you can find more suggested questions to ask or avoid during this evaluation, if you are having trouble with this task.

Speaking to Listening Ratio

Getting a better understanding of your speaking-to-listening ratio should be easy. All you need to do is ask your participant's one question: how often do I speak versus listen during a conversation? No need to request specific percentages, simply ask if you speak more or listen more when conversing.

Vocabulary and Use of Slang

You need to be as specific as possible when asking for an evaluation of your use of vocabulary and slang. Use these questions to get the answers you need:

- Do I use a lot of slang while I'm speaking?
- Do I often use proper English when speaking?
- Do I tend to speak like most people in my community or do I stand out?

Body Language

To get the most accurate description of what type body language you display during most conversations, ask several questions instead of one or two. Use these questions if you are having trouble figuring out what to ask:

- Do I use my hands a lot while I'm speaking?
- Do I make eye contact?
- Do I stand close to you during most our conversations, or do I tend to stand a least an arm length apart?
- Do I move my head a lot while I'm speaking?
- Do I typically have an assertive or aggressive posture while speaking or a more passive stance?

Frustration Limit's

When you're asking someone about your frustration limits, try to get answers that can be measured. Here are a few questions that should accomplish this task:

- How quickly do I get upset during an argument or debate? A few seconds, minutes, or longer?
- What are some common words or phrases that seem to get me riled up the most?
- How quickly do I walk away from a conversation when I disagree with the other person?

Tone

All questions related to tone should be very specific, but limited. For the purposes of this exercise, you should only have to ask these two questions to get what you need.

- When I'm talking, am I typically loud, moderate, or pretty quiet?
- When I'm arguing or debating am I typically loud, moderate, or pretty quiet?

Once all these questions are answered, compare your self-evaluation with your peer evaluation. Are they similar or very different? If they are different, don't feel too bad. Most people tend to see themselves in a way that differs from how everyone else sees them. While you may mean one thing when you speak, sometimes the other person may not completely understand what you are saying. The point of this exercise is to obtain an accurate assessment of the way you communicate with others, and that typically requires the help of others.

Now it is time to ask your spouse about your communication skills. To prevent another argument from occurring, don't make this conversation seem like an attempt to improve his or her communication skills. This exercise has everything to do with your contributions to miscommunication, not your spouse's. Your goal is to figure out what words or actions cause a negative reaction from your spouse, regardless of what topic is being discussed. Do this by asking this question: what do I say or do during our conversations that cause you to be upset or irritated? No matter how your spouse answers, do not react emotionally. This is not the time to criticize your spouse for being honest. If your spouse will not cooperate and refuses to offer a helpful answer to this question, explain the purpose of the question. Tell him or her that you are doing a self-evaluation related to your communication skills and would appreciate his or her input. If your spouse continues to reject your request, drop the topic and consider a less confrontational approach. You can do this by asking your spouse to fill out an evaluation sheet with the same questions you presented to your friends and family. You can also ask your spouse if your timing was bad and ask him or her to give an answer at a later time. If nothing works, and your spouse consistently refuses to talk to you about anything related to your marriage, you may need to consult a relationship counselor or some other third -party assistance. This exercise can only be successful if you have a spouse that is at least willing to answer a few questions. If there are serious unresolved issues that are preventing any conversations related to the marriage from occurring, following these instructions probably won't lead you to anything helpful. However, if your spouse is responsive to this question, compare his or her answer to your previous evaluations.

Is there any correlation between the responses you received from your spouse and peers? Do the words or actions that bother your spouse show up anywhere in your peer evaluations? When they do, you have confirmation of a habit that needs to be addressed. These communication habits are keeping you from being able to resolve conflicts with your spouse, and have nothing to do with being correct or incorrect. You've simply identified communication barriers between you and your spouse, and they need to be removed to reach your ultimate goal of increasing financial compatibility. Practice avoiding these habits before going into any financial debate to avoid disagreements related to communication issues. Once you are able to move beyond these issues, you will find it easier to have a discussion about financial matters. If you were not able to find any similarities between your spouse's responses and your peer evaluations, something isn't right. Why do the people that are closest to you have such different opinions about the way you communicate? It's not like you're comparing your associates and work friends with your spouse. These are the people that know the real you; therefore, there should be some similarities. When this happens, there can only be one reason for such different perspectives, you don't speak to your spouse like a friend or family. Work on avoiding the speaking habits that bother your spouse, and try to remember to speak to your spouse not only like a husband or wife, but also like a friend.

Now that you've worked on improving your marital communication skills, another major issue may still need to be addressed. While effective communication may no longer be a major issue, it is possible to still have some unpleasant perceptions of your spouse. You won't be able to increase or create financial compatibility with your spouse without some perception changes, especially if you perceive him or her as an obstacle or barrier between you and your lifestyle dreams. You may have never expected to feel this way about your spouse, but life experiences can lead to this change. When you were dating, your partner probably seemed like a good fit for you and your lifestyle ambitions. You felt he or she could add value to your life and wouldn't hold you back from achieving your dreams, even after marriage. The simple thought of a life together with your lover brought a smile to your face, and you were ready to take the next step: marriage. Then something changed after you got married. The person you fell in love with was no longer someone who would do everything to make sure your dreams come true. Gradually, your spouse seemed very interested in achieving his or her lifestyle goals, but lacked enthusiasm whenever your goals and aspirations are mentioned. It is as if your spouse stopped caring about your dreams and only wants to make you a part of his or her plans. This transition happens in most marriages because it is difficult to bridge the lifestyle goals of two different people together. Your goal during the next phase of resolving conflicts is to change this mindset.

Do you remember the conversations you had with your spouse when you were first dating or when you started growing a friendship? If you weren't teenagers, these conversations probably included some discussion of lifestyle ambitions and goals. You told him or her about what you wanted to do in life, the number of kids you wanted to have, and where you dreamed of living. Those conversations always seemed pleasant because they probably lacked one thing: negative responses or criticism.

Both of you only wanted to be an asset to each other's dreams, and made sure it was known. This is a common theme of the dating phase, and you need to incorporate it into your marriage. The hard part about doing this is letting go of past mistakes.

After living with your spouse for a year or two, bad habits become fully exposed. When these habits affect household financial matters, they are rarely forgotten, and this record of mistakes begins to overshadow optimism. Once consistent broken promises are added to these instances, a negative disposition also begins to grow. Over time, this is adds up to a lack of trust within the marriage, and the mindset needed to increase financial compatibility dissipates. Now is the time to overcome this mindset, and you can attempt to do so by following these steps:

Schedule a bi-annual dreams and aspirations date, which was described in "WHEN TWO BECOME ONE". Doing this at least twice per year will help to correlate positive emotions with financial discussions and reinforce trust.

You need to practice following through on all your small promises. When you tell your spouse that you will wash the dishes, clean up a room, pick up something from the store, take the children to the park, call during lunch, or any other small task, do it. Don't allow work or fatigue to excuse you from your promise. Delivering on these types of small promises helps to build trust within your relationship. Married couples often view these promises as small matters, but they are very important. Make a list of all the promises you make in a week and then check off the promises you've delivered on. If your sheet is not full of checks, it is time to step up your game. Try to improve your follow through as much as possible, and your spouse will begin to view you with more optimism, and may follow your lead.

Be patient with yourself and your spouse. Bad habits are not formed overnight and will not go away quickly. If your partner is willing to work on his or her bad habits, don't become an overseer of progression. It takes a lot of humility to admit faults and work on them. Pilling on criticism for lack of growth will likely slow down progression. Instead of focusing on your partner's progression, concentrate on where you are with improving your bad habits. This is not a race or contest to see who overcomes their bad habits first. You are in a lifetime partnership and need to be willing to wait out the process when your spouse is willing to make changes. If your spouse is not willing to change, you should still focus on yourself. It is not up to you to force this change; your spouse has to decide to change for him or herself. Otherwise, you may see short-term improvements, but long-term failure. If your spouse is not willing to compromise or work on his or her issues, there may be problems present that are too deep to improve by simply following these steps. In these instances, a third-party professional should be contacted for assistance.

Don't allow financial discrepancies to hinder intimacy. There is nothing worse than a marriage which lacks intimacy, and you need to fight hard to keep it. Do everything in your power to separate the two matters. If that means renting out a hotel room a few times per year because too much drama is tied to the house, go and do it. Outside of losing your home or committing a crime, you need to be willing to do anything to keep things sexy in your household. You know what your spouse likes better than anyone else, so don't let your anger cloud this knowledge. Financial disagreements do not justify a retraction of intimacy, even if those differences create stress. Remember, intimacy is not a reward for good behavior. It's an expression of love.

Create realistic expectations for you and your partner. Let go of all the preconceived ideas of what your spouse should be and accept what he or she is. By accepting your spouse for who he or she is, you are not agreeing that personal growth should not occur. You are just putting your relationship in its proper perspective. The goals you have for yourself and your spouse need to be tailored for less disappointment. If you are constantly let down by the lack of your spouse's ability to meet your ideals, it is unlikely that you will be able to observe small progression. We all need to be encouraged while we are striving to accommodate our mates and can't do this unless our partners are able to appreciate small progress. Over a period of time, these steps towards increased compatibility will become large leaps, but you must recognize them first.

When you and your spouse are not able to resolve these types of conflicts, it is time to search for third- party assistance. The assistance you are looking for shouldn't come from a family member, friend, or associate with no professional counseling credentials. You need to find someone who has experience. Sit down with your spouse and talk about the possibility of seeking marital counseling. If he or she agrees, make sure to pick a counselor that meets both of your approval. You can ask friends, family, and even religious brethren for recommendations, if needed. If keeping this matter private is a big concern, do your research on the internet, but be sure to double check all references you find. Websites like Yelp.com and FindaDoc.com may be able to assist you with this search, but don't forget to search the name of any doctors you are interested in for reviews and complaints. Wait until after you've spoken to a counseling specialist before you move forward with any other serious financial discussions. If your spouse refuses to seek the help of a counselor, ask him or her if about going alone. Though it may be ideal to have your spouse attend these sessions with you, don't allow his or her reluctance to keep you from getting help. These sessions could be the difference between divorce and a long-lasting marriage.

Another tool you can use to resolve your financially based marital conflicts is the numbers-based decision process. It works just like it's spelled out. Instead of making financial decisions based on a mix of emotions, mathematical equations will make the decision for you. It's very simple. Whenever you are not able to resolve your financial disagreements, break out the numbers and base the final decision on greatest wealth creation. Here is a simple equation to get you started:

Plan A asset increase – Plan A liability increase =

VS

Plan B asset increase – Plan B liability increase =

Here is an example of how you can use this formula:

Collin and Erica are trying to plan a kitchen remodel. Collin wants to knock down a wall, put new tile on the floor, purchase a granite counter-top, and replace the old cabinets. Erica wants to put new tile on the floor, purchase a granite counter-top, stain the old cabinets, and replace the gas stove with an electric stove. They agree on the floor and counter top upgrades, but can't seem to compromise on the other plans. Both plans are within their spending budget of $15,000, and they really want to get past these issues. To resolve this, they agree to go with the decision that will increase the value of their home the most. After consulting with an appraiser, they were able to gather the data needed to determine which plan would increase the home value the most. Collin's plan would cost $13,500 and increase the home value by $23,000. Erica's plan would cost $8,000 and increase the home value by $19,000. Based on the equation above, Collin's plan would result in a $9,500 net worth increase and Erica's plan would result in an $11,000 net worth increase with less money spent. Using the numbers-based decision making process would result in Erica's plan being chosen. Collin shouldn't be too upset because the entire household gained something from this decision. However, if their conflict was related to something that can't be measured by dollars, such as the benefit of taking a vacation, small purchases, concerts, then this process would not work as a stand-alone. It would still be a good tool, but the other unmeasurable factors must also be considered.

Creating equal-benefit, win-win resolutions is one of the most efficient ways to conquer marital conflicts. Equal-benefit, win-win resolutions ensure all parties involved in a dispute benefit equally from the resolution. It slightly differs from the common-known, win-win resolution because it does not allow either party to obtain a measurable benefit that exceeds the value of the other. Without the equal benefit factor, one person could end up with a benefit worth $20,000 and the other receives a benefit worth $5,000, which would create an unbalanced win-win. This lack of balance might be acceptable for a short period of time, but is likely to create long-term resentment. In some cases, one person may receive a benefit that is slightly more valuable than the other, but the difference should be no more than five percent to stay within the equal benefit boundaries.

7

THE CHILDREN EFFECT

There is nothing more beautiful than coming together with your spouse to create a new life inspired by love. It is truly a life-altering moment. You're in love with your spouse, and the desire to bring a child into your world with him or her is stronger than ever. The world around you may be full of chaos, but your household is truly in a good place. You're ready, and have taken the necessary steps to add to your family. This is the ideal process most people would like to go through before having children, but it doesn't always work out that way. Today, many parents don't bring their child into this world through marriage, and sometimes, they had children within a failed marriage. The children you bring into this world will be a blessing to your life, and are too precious to ever compare to anything tangible, but they will come with a price. What that price will be is up to you. Will you let your love for your children lead to the end of your marriage? Are you willing to sacrifice all of your personal dreams for the sake of your children? How about your financial stability? Should you have children if you're barely able to take care of yourself? Are you willing to allow your children to live in financial distress and learn in unsatisfactory environments because of your financial issues? These are just a few of the personal questions you need to ask yourself when preparing to have children. If you don't, you are not only increasing the potential of limiting social and economic opportunities for your child, but you are also putting your marriage in danger. However, if you've already had children and didn't plan well for their arrival, it's never too late to address these issues.

All parents know about the difficulties and joys that come with raising children, but many don't know what price they are willing to pay for taking on the task of raising their children. How could anyone know what these limits are or if they even exist? Until people are put in situations that will test their limits, it is impossible for them to be completely certain of how they will react. This uncertainty will always be present in your life, but that doesn't mean you shouldn't think about them ahead of time. Now is the time to consider the cost of adding children to your life, even if you've already had children. Here's some information to get you started:

According to the Department of Agriculture, it will take $241,080 to raise a child born in the year 2012 until he or she is seventeen years old. These figures account for the costs of clothing, sheltering, feeding, educating, and other expenses related to raising a child in the United States. While this figure is only an estimated average, and doesn't include the costs of providing for adult children, it is still good to use for the purpose of examining the costs of raising children. If the average cost of raising one child is roughly one quarter of a million dollars, think about the impact three or four children will have on the average U.S. household. You could easily find yourself spending over one million dollars to raise all of your children. Now compare that figure to the median U.S. household income in 2012: $51,017. Once other expenses related to the home, taxes, automobiles, food, and insurances are paid, little is left for the average household to cover these child related expenses. If you were to divide $241,080 over seventeen years, the costs would average out to $14,181 per year, which accounts for nearly twenty-eight percent of the average U.S. household total gross income. While these figures may seem somewhat reasonable, it is far from that. In the real world, child care costs are not evenly distributed throughout seventeen years. The first four or five years of a child's life are typically more expensive than the other twelve to thirteen years.

Paying for daycare and after-school care is difficult for most American households. These services can range from $100 per week for each child to $461 per week for each child, and in some areas, it's more expensive. That equates to an annual $5,200 - $24,000 in daycare or after-school care costs per child. Even at the lower end of the spectrum, this service will cost the average U.S. household ten percent of their annual income. Multiplying these figures by four years results in $20,800 of the $241,080 needed to raise a child going towards these services, which is roughly nine percent of the total. That's a big hit to the average American household. This may not have been so important thirty plus years ago, when it was more popular for at least one parent to stay home while the other worked, but modern society is much different. Since 1967, there has been at least a twenty percent decline of stay-at-home mothers in U.S. households. This is a reflection of an increase in mothers choosing to remain or become a part of the U.S. workforce instead of staying home over the last forty years. Women did not have as many opportunities to find work in previous decades, but today they are plentiful, and many mothers prefer to pursue career ambitions versus staying home. However, over the last two to three years, an increasing number of mothers and fathers are choosing to remain home for a few years to eliminate the need for such services and avoid the costs. Some employers also offer child-care assistance to help their employees cover these expenses, but it usually isn't enough to outweigh the financial benefit of staying home. There is some indirect relief being offered by employers through work from home programs. Though it is nearly impossible to work efficiently and take care of an infant from home, it does allow for some space and time to manage both. Coming out of these first few years without too much financial damage must be your goal; otherwise, you will pay sorely in the future.

Once your child is no longer an infant or toddler, the cost of care begins to decrease until he or she becomes a pre-teen. As pre-teens, children begin to eat almost as much as adults. Their clothes are more expensive. Extra-curricular activities become more expensive. Birthday requests are more costly. Social activities are a must, but the children are too young to actually get a job. These children don't come cheap. They are going to literally eat your budget alive. The sad part about this stage of their lives is the speed in which it will transition to even higher costs.

Outside of all direct financial impacts, children will affect financial compatibility within their household by attempting to play parents against each other. Their mission is to get whatever they want, by any means necessary. If your marriage has to suffer for the sake of the newest video-gaming system or apparel, so be it. They expect you, as a parent, to overcome such trivial matters. Children want what they want and don't expect to have to wait for it. Though they will bring these challenges, it is up to you, the parent, to maintain the financial and emotional balance of the household. Children that don't get all A's and B's on their report cards will make this task easy. They are giving you a way out of granting their wishes by not performing well in school. Those that get straight A's are the ones that make this task difficult. It isn't easy to refuse the request of a child that is well-behaved, an excellent student, and responsible. They do the things you ask of them and deserve to be rewarded, but at what price?

Rewarding children for good behavior should never usurp maintaining financial compatibility within your marriage. If you're going to take a financial hit to reward your children, the decision to do so must be mutual. When you decide to prolong a reward for good behavior, blame for the circumstances leading to this delay must be avoided. These are the "all in" or "all out" decisions that must be made in complete unity. While you and your spouse may not totally agree on the final decision, you both must stand firm on the final decision. Embracing the opposite could damage your marriage beyond repair. Think about it for a moment: what's the worst that could happen from rewarding your child and forsaking your marriage? Marriages don't end because of such a small thing, or do they? If you've never heard of this occurring, here's a story that will illustrate this reality:

In the fall of 2002, Eric and Susan were in the midst of celebrating their ninth year of marriage, when Susan presented Eric with a surprise. She revealed that she was pregnant with their second child, and Eric was ecstatic. They already had a beautiful seven year old daughter, Kim. Susan and Eric were looking forward to the possibility of having a son with this latest pregnancy. Kim was even excited to become a big sister, or at least she appeared to feel this way. Whenever Eric and Susan asked Kim how she felt about becoming a big sister, she responded with a big smile and dance. They immediately began to prepare for their newest addition by making plans to convert the home office into a nursery and increasing their savings. After Susan surpassed her first trimester, the family decided it was time to let their relatives know about the pregnancy. They invited everyone to the house for a spring cookout, and announced the good. Everyone was filled with joy after hearing the announcement and wanted to know the gender of their soon-to-arrive baby. Eric and Susan decided to hold off on knowing the sex of the child until a week before the delivery date. As that date grew closer, Kim became needier and sought more attention from Eric and Susan. She knew her sibling was coming and felt the need to ensure her parent's still loved her. Eric and Susan did all they could to ensure Kim of their love for her. They spent less time watching television and initiated more family outings. They redecorated Kim's room while building the new nursery. Susan even made sure to remind Kim how much she loved her every night, but they couldn't stop what was coming. One week before Susan's delivery date, she and Eric found out they were having a boy, and Eric could not hide his excitement. He jumped up and threw his fist in the air once he heard the great news. Kim wasn't as enthusiastic. She just did her best to smile and not seem upset. Secretly, she had been hoping for a little sister. Once Susan gave birth to her new baby boy, Nathan, she couldn't get out of the hospital soon enough. She was anxious to get home and get settled in. Two days after the delivery, they went home, and Kim immediately wanted all her mother's attention. Over the next several months, she did everything she could to take attention away from her new little brother. She behaved well in school and got all A's. She did all her chores and cleaned up after herself. Kim even offered to read bedtime stories to her brother just to get in between him and her parents. Eric and Susan noticed this change in Kim and didn't know what to do about it. Without talking to Susan, Eric decided to use material rewards to help Kim feel more loved. This was the way his parents dealt with similar issues, and he felt it would work with Kim. Whenever he could, Eric would take Kim out to the toy store and buy her whatever she asked for. Once Susan found out about what Eric was doing, she was upset. Susan felt Eric's solution was irresponsible considering all the money they recently spent to build the nursery and the new expenses that came with taking care of their infant son. She voiced these concerns to Eric, but he disagreed with her take on the situation. Eric told Susan that he had everything under control and not to worry. While she was pregnant, he handled most of the finances and ensured her that they could afford to spoil their well-behaved daughter. Despite

Eric's pleas, Susan disagreed with his actions and asked him to stop. Eric agreed, but secretly kept buying things for his daughter and hid them in the garage. Kim also knew her mother didn't agree with these shopping trips, and agreed to always keep her new toys in the garage. She didn't want to upset her mother, but she wasn't going to give up her new gifts either.

A few months passed by and Susan began to notice a something different about the garage. There seemed to be more boxes than she could remember in there, and she decided to take a look into a few of them. Susan finds most of the toys and games Eric secretly purchased for Kim and became enraged. She couldn't believe Eric would betray her trust and called him to talk about it. Eric was at work when Susan called, and could hear the anger in here tone. Before she could explain why she was angry, he told her that he was in a meeting and would talk to her once he got home. His work day was ending in the next forty-five minutes, so he figured she could wait that long to say whatever she needed to say. He assumed Susan found out about the toys and was upset because he couldn't think of any other reason she would be angry. Once he got home, Susan was so anxious to let Eric know how she was feeling that she met him as soon as he pulled up in the driveway. She immediately began to voice her displeasure with his antics while holding baby Nathan in her arms. Eric then asks Susan if they could talk about this in the house, so the neighbors wouldn't see them argue. She agreed and went in the house, and then put Nathan in his crib before continuing the conversation. She started fussing at Eric again, and he interjected with an apology. He explained the intentions of his actions, but was sorry for lying to her. To solve this issue, Eric decided he would no longer lie about the expenditures, but wouldn't stop buying things for Kim when he felt like it. Obviously, Susan was not happy about this. The apology meant nothing to her if it didn't come with a change in action. She decided to just drop to the topic because these purchases didn't seem to put their financial security at risk. Eric was satisfied with the outcome of this argument, and continued to buy gifts for his daughter. For the next several years, Eric began to use this philosophy with all the household financial matters. He began to make investment choices without Susan's consent. He accepted credit offers without her knowledge. He even upgraded his car without talking to her. As long as he wasn't making decisions that hurt the household, he felt okay about them. Susan grew tired of this behavior and began to resent Eric. In her mind, he was being selfish and didn't care much about her feelings regarding their finances.

After seven years of this behavior, one of Eric's investment choices came back to haunt him. Unknowingly, he invested $30,000 in a Ponzi scheme, and lost it all. He'd previously told Susan that this money was going to be used for Kim's college fund. Kim had just been accepted to Duke University when he lost their savings. She was certain her dad and mom had enough money saved to cover Duke's tuition costs and couldn't wait to attend her favorite university. She had been a Blue Devil's fan since she started high school and couldn't wait to become a student. Once Kim and Susan found out the money was gone, they were devastated. Susan was especially upset because she heard about this Ponzi scheme when Eric first decided to invest with this fraudulent company, but he never told her about the details of this investment. She couldn't believe Eric could be so irresponsible. Kim didn't bother to apply to other schools because she was certain that she would be attending Duke, and had to rush to apply to other schools.

Susan's years of resentment all came out at once. She packed up her and the kid's things and temporarily moved into her parent's house. She was completely fed up with Eric's behavior, and their marriage was in serious trouble. After cooling down for a few days, Susan went back to the house to discuss things with Eric. He was very apologetic about making such a bad decision, but felt her reaction was a bit extreme. This was the only serious financial mistake he'd made during their marriage and felt she was being too hard on him. Susan told him that she would only come back if he waited for her approval before making any new financial decisions. He felt this one mistake didn't warrant such changes and told her they should try to discuss the matter again in a few weeks. She agreed and went back to her parents' house. A few weeks passed and she received a call on her cell phone from Visa. Eric listed her cell as an alternated number if he couldn't be reached. They told her that her they were past due on one of the credit cards and requested a payment. She told the bill collector that she would call Eric and see what's going on. Instead of calling Eric, she decided to meet him at the house because they were scheduled to meet based on their previous discussion. Once she arrived, Eric met her at the door with a surprised expression. He knew something was wrong because Susan had her armed cross and appeared to be ready for an argument. Susan immediately began to question Eric about his past-due credit card bill. She tells him about the call she received and wanted to know why he never revealed the existence of this account in the past. Eric scratched his head and took a deep breath before offering Susan an explanation. He went on to explain the details behind him getting the credit card and its delinquent status. It turned out that Eric used the card to pay for Kim's graduation expenses and class dues. He was attempting to make up for his past mistake and got the credit card to help with these efforts. Unfortunately, his efforts backfired because he was unable to keep up with the payments. Susan had reached her limit. She no longer could tolerate Eric's secrets and his unwillingness to change. She told him what her final decision would be regarding the status of their marriage. Susan wanted a divorce, though Eric wanted to work things out. Their marriage was essentially over, and it can partially be blamed on a lack of financial compatibility.

I've heard hundreds of stories like the one you just read throughout my career in finance. Not only are the problems Eric and Susan experienced realistic, they are quite common. The biggest problems were a lack of humility from Eric and a lack of forgiveness by Susan. In the beginning, Eric just wanted to reward their daughter for being a well-behaved child and show her the love he felt she needed. This desire to please a child led to the demise of the marriage and any financial compatibility that existed.

Children aren't the only people that can cause a breakdown of marital unity; parents that forsake all of their personal desires to focus on their children also contribute. Sacrificing financial stability and lifestyle goals for the sake of investing in the future of your children should always be a mutual decision. It isn't easy to give up on lifestyle and financial ambitions because of the responsibilities that accompany parenthood. In the public, we all would like to be known as parents that are willing to sacrifice anything for our children, but in private, we are more torn about this issue. If you give up on your dreams and try to live through your kids, severe depression and regret could overtake your mind. If you put too much of your efforts into your own dreams, the relationship you have with your kids and spouse could suffer. What do you do in this situation? The answer is simpler than the work it will take to reach it: balance. You need to find a happy medium between pursuit of personal and mutual lifestyle goals and parental responsibilities. There is no perfect formula for you to follow to get to obtain this balance. Where your balance resides is totally dependent on the ability to understand yourself. Your friends can't tell you what it should be. Your parents and family can't tell you where it should be. Not even your spouse can determine ideal balance. This is one of the few moments you should utilize your emotions for help. If after one day you feel slighted because you spent most of the day caring for the needs of others, make a note of the activities you did. How would spending eight hours at work, four hours taking care of things for the kids, three hours doing things for your spouse, and the other nine hours eating and sleeping cause you to feel? If you'd feel slighted, try taking away an hour for one or two of those activities and do something for yourself. Make notes and adjustments like this for at least three weeks, and you will begin to find your happy medium. Once you find it or begin to get closer to it, let your family know about your findings. Ask them to help you with maintaining this balance, and let them know how important it is to your mental and physical health. While the well-being of your children and spouse are very important, you are not any good to them if you are living in a state of depression or sadness. Your family wants you to be happy, and your happiness helps them.

There are also some other members of the household that can cause financial problems, pets. You would be surprised how often I've heard couples argue about how much money is spent on their pets. Similar to differing opinions about child care, couples often had different beliefs about the amount of care that should be provided for pets. Some people were raised to believe pets are like children, and were willing to spend whatever money was needed to ensure the survival and great upkeep of their pet. Others believed keeping their pet alive was sufficient, and weren't willing to spend more money than what covered the essentials. To ensure these differences don't lead to arguments, couples must talk about them and fully understand the costs associated with caring for a pet. The best place to begin is with the basic costs of pet ownership.

Food: All pets eat. There is no way of getting around this expense, and understanding how much your future or current pet eats is a must. The bigger the size of your pet, the more money you will need to set aside for pet food. It's that simple. Feeding a small fish typically requires spending $20 - $40 annually, but a large dog would be more in the range of $1,800 - $2,500. Be sure to know how much it will cost to feed your future pet before agreeing to ownership. If you already have a pet and your spouse is a non-pet owner, make sure he or she is fully aware of these costs.

Toys/Treats: Any good pet owner will tell you that pets need to be entertained, and that means buying toys. Pets that live in small environments like a fish tank or cage may only require one-time purchases to cover this expense, but most others may need a new toy each month. Depending on pet type, expect to spend anywhere between $25 -$200 annually for toys.

Recurring Medical Expenses: Like humans, many pets need annual or bi-annual medical checkups. Pets that are relatively healthy will only require minimal care, and can be easily planned for. Typical annual medical expenses will usually range from $80 - $450, but could be higher if your pet becomes injured and has to receive continual treatment. Be sure to research which common disabilities your pet is most susceptible to.

Grooming: Some pets require regular grooming due to health needs and for home sanitations purposes. More hair leads to more trips to see a pet groomer. This service can cost anywhere from twenty to eighty dollars per trip. Some pet owners can offset these costs by doing the grooming themselves, but most shouldn't take on this responsibility. Grooming requires skill, and not everyone can perform this task with care.

Shelter: All pets need to be sheltered, and your home by itself isn't always enough. Be sure to know how much it will costs to provide some type of housing for your pet and how often you will need to upgrade it. Some pets grow very quickly and will need their cage, tank, or barn adjusted or expanded to accommodate their new size. Others simply require a one-time purchase due to their lack of growth. These purchases can range from twenty dollars to one hundred and fifty dollars.

Outside of basic expenses, you also need to talk about pet lifestyle expenses. Most pets lifestyle expenses are a direct reflection of their owner's lifestyle choices. Pet owners that like to exercise typically want their four-legged pets to be walked or exercised just as often. Those that frequently travel usually purchase traveling items so their pets can accompany them. Owners that are into fashion are likely to want their pets to look fashionable too. Talk to your spouse about all expectations related to pet lifestyle to ensure these expenses are properly planned for. If you decide against openly discussing pet care, you can look forward to some unwanted stress.

8

GETTING OUT OF DEBT TOGETHER

Some people will leave a marriage when financial stress shows its ugly face. These individuals can't deal with the prospects of financial struggle and prefer to move on by themselves. Others choose to stay, and work through these difficulties. If you've made it this far in the book, don't doubt yourself. You are a part of the group that prefers to work things out, and this was written for you.

There is no sure way to guarantee your spouse will put forth as much effort as you while attempting to create financial stability. It is not certain you will match his or her efforts either. There is only one aspect of working towards household financial freedom that you can count on. The efforts of both you and your spouse will be needed to reach your goals. This is the mindset you will need to reach the finish line. Mistakes will occur during this process. Your spouse will let you down from time to time. There will even be moments when you feel like your efforts were done in vain, but you must not let them change your mindset. To build this level of consistency, you need to practice using it. Take advantage of the small disappointments within your daily life by using them for practice. When you notice someone within your household hasn't taken care of his or her cleaning duties, take care of their task yourself without being asked. Let the person responsible for the task know that you took care of it and are not looking for reciprocation. If your spouse is supposed to pick up some food from the local grocery store, take off from work early or adjust your schedule to be able to do it yourself. Don't use these efforts as a negotiating tool during arguments or disputes. Don't make your spouse feel obligated to return the favor. Simply complete the task and let him or her know that it is done. By doing this, you are improving your comfort with unselfish sacrifice. Do this at least once per week until it doesn't feel uncomfortable while you are working on getting out of debt.

Now that your mind is ready for the challenges that await you, it is time to start the process of getting out of debt as a couple. The first thing you need to do is identify all of your debts, if you haven't already. This task can be difficult for some because of a long habit of ignoring bills and bill collectors, but it can still be done. By utilizing your personal credit reports, old mail, old emails, caller ID, and checking unheard voicemail messages, you should be able to identify almost all your debts.

There are three major credit reporting agencies that you can use to identify most of your outstanding debts: Equifax, Experian, and Trans Union. At least once a year, you can obtain a free copy of your personal credit report from these agencies. These reports will list your reported debts and creditor contact information, which can be useful when incorrect data is reported or you're not sure who to contact about your outstanding debt. This is the most useful method to account for all your outstanding debt. However, you need to be sure to obtain a credit report for you and your spouse. Though you may have mutual debts, it is highly likely that each of you have stand-alone debts too.

Opening your unopened mail and emails can also be very useful when trying to identify your outstanding debts. These paper and electronic records often contain more current information regarding your debts than personal credit reports. While credit reporting agencies update on a monthly basis, paper and electronic mail can be distributed daily or weekly. Open these letters and match them up with your credit reports to identify any differences. If everything aligns, you can disregard the letters, unless they contain more up-to-date creditor contact information. Letters that don't match up with your credit reports need to be researched for accuracy. The last thing you want to do is pay a bill that isn't really yours. There are plenty of scams artists who utilize paper and electronic mail to steal your information. Don't take any shortcuts doing your homework when things don't match up simply because it's a tedious task. Your due diligence will be rewarded.

If you are like most people with debt problems, you've probably ignored creditor calls and messages. Like your unopened letters, these unanswered calls and messages may be the leads you need while trying to identify all of your outstanding debts. While mail is sent weekly or monthly, creditors call just about every day. Compare these missed calls and voicemails with the contact information in your credit reports and mail. This is another situation where you must be on the lookout for potential scams. Utilize search engines to identify any negative or fraud reports regarding these numbers. Typically, all you will need to do is conduct a search using a phone number, but you can also search the business name when possible. Don't callback any of these numbers until you're sure they are connected to a legitimate organization. If you call these numbers and feel uneasy about providing personal information, only give your name and ask for the purpose of their previous calls.

Once you and your spouse have identified all outstanding debts, categorize them based on importance, delinquency, and outstanding balance. First, rank your debts based on level of importance and include the minimal monthly payments associated with each debt.

Debts that are linked to household necessities like mortgage loans, open mortgage lines of credit, auto loans, child support, and student loans should be ranked the highest. Other credit card loans, medical bills, and personal loans should follow. The lowest-ranking debts should be your collections bills that are already charged off or not with the original lender. While these bills are still important, they often won't affect your ability to provide shelter, clothing, transportation, and food for your household. After you're done with this list, move on to creating a new list of your debts with delinquency, minimal monthly payment, and balance information. Start by listing the debt that is the furthest past due and include its outstanding balance and minimal monthly payment. The last debt on this list should be the debt which is closest to or is a current status.

Next, take these lists and compare them to your current monthly net income and total savings. Subtract all your monthly food, utilities, insurance, clothing, and medication expenses from your total monthly net income before moving forward. Starting at the top of your ranked importance debt list, identify how much of your remaining monthly net income is able to cover the minimum monthly payments associated with these debts. If your remaining income is able to cover all the monthly payments on this list, skip to the next paragraph related to your delinquent debt list. However, if your monthly net income runs out before the end of the list, draw a line under the last debt where the monthly payment could be paid. This line is the maximum monthly bill payment limit. Reaching this limit means you are not able to pay the monthly minimum payments of any of your remaining debts without the use of savings or credit. If you have funds in your savings accounts that can be easily obtained, use these funds to identify which monthly payments can be covered after the maximum monthly bill payment limit has been reached. Draw another line under the last debt that could be

covered with your savings funds if you couldn't reach the
end of your list. This line is called the savings–based,
maximum monthly bill payment limit. Put this list to the
side for now, but keep it close. We will need to revisit this
list at a later time.

Now you need to compare your updated
importance rank list with your delinquency list. Where do
the most delinquent debts appear on your importance rank
list? Are they the furthest past due? Are most of the
delinquent accounts found at the bottom or middle of
your importance rank list? Knowing the location of your
most delinquent debts within your need-based debts
rankings is a very important part of this debt -reduction
process. If your most delinquent debts fall amongst the
least important debts, it is likely that your debt reduction
plan will not be solely based on increasing your cash flow.
There is more room to consider long-term debt reduction,
net worth increase, and increasing savings. If the opposite
is true, increasing your cash flow will be a higher priority.
You also need to pay attention to your income and saving-
based monthly payment limits, and compare them to your
delinquency list. Are you running out of money before the
monthly payments for the furthest delinquent accounts can
be paid? Are you able to pay the minimal monthly
payments for your most delinquent accounts, but not the
most current accounts? Knowing the answer to these
questions will also heavily impact your debt reduction plan.
If you are running out of monthly income or savings
before you can pay your most delinquent accounts, solving
this problem will be at the heart of your plan. If you are
able to pay your most delinquent accounts but not the
most current accounts, this issue must be resolved.

The total balances and monthly payments of these
debts must also be examined before you formally create a
debt-reduction plan. This is where most people have the
most problems. Some financial experts suggest paying
down debts with the highest interest rates first. Others

suggest paying off debts with the highest balances first. To determine which method is best for you, the previous analysis must be factored into this one. If you are experiencing a cash flow problem, meaning you don't have enough household income and savings to cover the minimum payments for all your outstanding debts, increasing your cash flow is the top priority. Paying off the highest outstanding balances before anything else is an inefficient practice for your circumstances. You need to eliminate as many minimum monthly payments as possible before thinking about paying of high balances. Do this by figuring out where your money will work best for you. Ignore all debts that are with third-party collectors or below your monthly payment limits. They can be addressed after you've improved your cash flow. You need to identify the accounts you are currently paying that can be paid of the fastest and have the highest minimum payments, without losing a necessity. To be clear, these necessities are your home, food, power, clothing, and some forms of transportation. Be sure to contact your creditors to see if it is possible to reduce your monthly payments. Some creditors will have to close your cards to do so, while others may reduce your interest rate without penalty. They might also suggest you contact a credit counseling company for additional assistance, but be careful. Working with these organizations could mean closing all of your credit card accounts. While this may not be an issue for those experiencing extreme financial hardship, others should be aware. Here is an example of how this process would work after all monthly payments have been reduced:

Melissa's Monthly Debts:

Loan	Minimum Payment	Total Balance
Mortgage	$1200.00	$250,000
Car Loan	$520.00	$27,000
Visa	$300.00	$17,000
MasterCard	$150.00	$12,000
Personal Loan	$150.00	$600.00

*In this scenario, assume all credit card, mortgage, and personal loans are thirty days past due. The auto loan is sixty days past due.

Considering all the debts in this scenario, the personal loan should be the account paid down most aggressively. If Melissa skipped one monthly payment on her Visa and MasterCard accounts, and used those funds to pay off her personal loan; she would immediately increase her monthly cash flow by $150.00. Keep in mind, Melissa currently has several collections bills and severely delinquency accounts. This may not be the best action for someone with no past due accounts; however, it works for Melissa. Over the next three months, she would be able to bring her Visa and MasterCard back to a thirty day delinquency status.

I know what some of you are thinking. Why do that and get two sixty day marks on your credit? Couldn't she just pay her minimal payments for the next four months and increase her cash flow by $150.00 in five months? Yes, she very well could have used this method, but a very important factor in this scenario is being ignored: risk. Melissa doesn't have enough income or savings to pay any other debts, which indicates her lack of savings or residual income. Would it be wise for her to delay this cash flow increase for four to five months when she could encounter unexpected expenses in the interim? Most people encounter unexpected expenses like emergency doctor visits, car repairs, speeding or parking tickets, gas price increases, and food price increases at least once every three months. When these things happen, they cause further damage to an already stressful situation. One of these expenses could cause her to fall one payment behind one of her credit card payments, and delay her cash flow increase by an additional month. She would be better off increasing her cash flow immediately. Melissa doesn't have the ability to pay her way out of being sixty days past due on her auto loan; therefore, another short-term sixty day mark on her credit cards will not cause significant damage to her credit score. What's more important at this point, short-term changes to her credit score or increasing her cash flow? While it may take her a few years to significantly increase her credit score, her cash flow is more important. This is why one formula doesn't work for all people. Be careful to consider all these factors while creating your plan. Your cash flow is very important if you are not able to pay all of your debts. A short-term debt reduction plan focused on cash flow increase should be used until the ability to consistently save money on a monthly basis has been achieved. Once this level of savings is in place, it is safe to transition into a new total debt-reduction plan.

When reducing your total household debt is the focus, all outstanding debts need to be addressed. While some debts may have been temporarily ignored during the cash flow increase stage, now they need to be addressed. All of the information gathering that took place a few steps back will now be used. It is time to create a plan of attack, and the goal is to reduce as much of your total debt as possible. Begin this phase of planning by figuring out which debt payback scheme will be used.

The credit score impact, debt-reduction plan eliminates debt while steadily increasing your credit score. This plan is perfect for households that want to re-enter the credit market within the next three to four years. In order for this plan to be effective, the following rules must be followed:

- All credit accounts that are current must remain current.
- No account can be allowed to progress into a lien or judgment.
- Collection accounts that are older than five years should not be prioritized over any other account.
- Minimizing credit utilization (limits vs. balance) must be a top priority.
- Accounts that are currently delinquent must not be allowed to charge off.

Create or download a budgeting sheet that accounts for all your household monthly income and expenses. List the total balance and minimum monthly payment of each debt next to where it is listed. At this point, your total monthly income should already exceed your total monthly expenses. If it doesn't, go back to the cash flow increase phase. Next, use your delinquency list to determine which past due debts can be brought up to date the fastest. Use at least seventy-five percent of your bottom line (total income minus total expenses) to bring your most delinquent accounts current. If you have several accounts with the same level of delinquency, prioritize these accounts based on the speed in which you are able to bring the account current. The accounts you can bring current the fastest should be paid first. Use the remaining twenty-five percent of your bottom line to increase your savings. Repeat this process until all non-collection

accounts are current. One all accounts are up to date,
begin to aggressively pay down the household's revolving
debts with the highest interest rates. Revolving debts are
debts with open-ended terms and monthly payments based
on total balance. These are typically credit card accounts.
Maintain the same formula used previously: seventy-five
percent of your bottom line, while paying down these
accounts. While this is happening, research your options
for refinancing all auto and mortgage loans. If you or your
spouse has an above average credit score, feel free to apply
for a refinanced loan with a maximum two lenders if your
secured loan rates are minimally three percent higher than
the national average loan rate. This doesn't mean you go
searching for a second mortgage. You are just looking to
transfer debt to another lender for the purpose of lowering
your interest rates. Once your revolving debt balances are
paid down to ten to twenty percent of their credit line,
shift your aggressive payments to any accounts that were
sent to a collections agency within the past three years.

Dealing with collection agencies and law firms can
be annoying, but it is necessary. All fears and concerns
must be overcome. These collectors need us to pay our
debts just as much as we need to pay them off. Collections
agencies purchase our debts from the original lender, and
they want to make a profit from their purchase. We
shouldn't avoid collectors just because of their attempts to
intimidate us. The consequences of not dealing with these
collectors can be far worse than simply speaking with
them. We don't want to check our bank accounts and find
out our hard earned money has been intercepted.
Collectors are filing small claims lawsuits more than ever
before. Not honoring a court summons results in either
liens or even bench warrants. Many people have been
pulled over by state troopers for speeding and ended up
going to jail for failure to appear in court. This could put
jobs and reputations at risk. Another bad choice is to hire
someone to settle debts, unless absolutely necessary. The

most common choice for representation is settlement agencies. Settlement agencies negotiate deals with collectors to lower debt balances. They claim to be able to lower overall debt by twenty to fifty percent and make sure all the harassing calls stop. Settlement companies claim to hire the best debt negotiators in the world. Their so-called "experts" are trained to get the best deals. This sounds really good until all the fine print is revealed. They forget to tell potential customers how much of their money is being put aside for profits. There is no mention of the collectors' ability to file a lawsuit working with them. Settlement agents never tell customers they have no leverage when negotiating with collectors. Why would a third party have more leverage than the person responsible for the debt? This just doesn't make sense. They are really just an expensive middle man and can cause more harm than good. These are for profit organizations, and they are not in business just to help people with debt problems. Unfortunately, many people find this out the hard way. Once an agreement is signed, there is no turning back. Terminating a contract with most settlement agencies will not result in a full refund.

Once you've taken care of the collections accounts, it is time to aggressively pay down your mortgage, student, and auto loans. Unlike the other loans, paying down these loans will take larger additional payments. Mortgage loan interest takes away more income from American households than any other debt. Paying your fifteen or thirty-year loan down is essential to increasing the total household net worth and reaching financial freedom. Try to make at least six additional full payments per year. If you can't do that, come as close as possible. Your auto loans may not impact your long-term earnings like mortgage loans do, but they should still be paid down aggressively. Try making an additional full payment every three months and add more as your income increases or your overall debt decreases. Doing this will not only increase your overall net worth;, it will cause your credit score to skyrocket.

The other debt payback strategy your household can follow is the net worth growth plan. This plan is all about eliminating household debt and has little regard for credit scores. It is an ideal plan for families focused on long term-financial goals and retirement. Similar to the credit score impact plan, there are rules that must be followed for this plan to be effective:

- Paying down loans with the largest interest charges must be the top priority.
- New mortgage loans should not be opened until the total household net worth is at least fifty percent higher than the total household yearly income.
- There should be no more than one auto loan per household, unless there were two or more when you started this plan.
- Never focus on debt elimination so much that you don't enjoy life. This process can become addictive, but life is too short not to have fun.

The first step in creating a net worth growth plan is to fill out a budgeting sheet. Make sure to include all your debts, their total balances, monthly payments, and interest rates. Also, include your total household income and savings. Once all the numbers are tallied,; make sure you've calculated your total monthly bottom line (total monthly income minus total monthly expenses). If you don't have any income left over after subtracting your monthly expenses, this plan isn't for you. Go back to the cash flow increase based plan. However, if you have enough money in your savings accounts (401k, regular savings, investment retirement account) to cover at least six months of bill payments, it is okay to stick with this plan. Next to each listed interest rate, note the current amount of interest being paid for each debt. Use an online amortization calculator or an interest-rate calculator to help with gathering these figures. Identify the debt with the highest interest charges and begin to aggressively pay it down. Use up to seventy-five percent of your bottom line money to work towards paying this debt down, and use the other twenty-five percent for savings. You can also transfer this debt to an account with a lower annual percentage rate, if possible, and attack another debt with high interest charges. As long as the terms are not extended, feel free to explore this option through the use of your 401k, IRA, or a consolidation loan. Just make sure to only take loans out of the investment accounts to avoid early withdrawal fees. Keep repeating these pay-down actions until your net worth has increased by at least twenty percent. If you care to go further, don't stop, but don't forget to enjoy your life along the way.

No matter which plan you choose to follow, there is one habit that must be overcome to reach the finish line: inconsistency. This habit has ruined financial plans for centuries. It has led to household's faltering. Nations have gone broke because of it. Businesses have closed when it is not embraced. Inconsistency has always been the number one enemy to any financial plan, but a fix to this problem has always been available. What is this fix? It's called rewarding good behavior in a responsible manner.

When you were children, why did you behave well in school and try to get good grades? Why did you do your chores and come in the house on time? While fear certainly played a role, something else typically motivated you to try harder and do better. It was the reward for this good behavior, and you still look forward to it as an adult. You want to be rewarded with bonuses and raises when you consistently perform your job at a high level. You want to be rewarded with affection when you do something nice for your spouse. You even desire to be rewarded when you raise your children to be successful. This desire can be used to encourage consistency when trying to follow a budgeting plan. All you need to do is include incentives in your financial plan based on your breaking points. What is a breaking point? These are the consistent moments that you stop following your plans. If you can only stick to a budget for three weeks without cheating, you have a three week breaking point. When you begin to cheat, you've reached your breaking point. Try your best to identify these breaking points and create incentives based on their frequency. These incentives can come in the form of a new pair of shoes, a movie night, a short vacation, or anything else you desire that doesn't cause a setback. Be sure not to spend too much money, which is any amount that sets your plan back by more than one month. If you find yourself cheating every five weeks, include a five week incentive in your plan. Once you've grown beyond those five weeks, move the incentives to every six weeks, and continue to move forward until you're satisfied with your growth. These rewards will keep you on track, but don't incent yourself too much. You don't want to find yourself moving at a snail's pace because your rewards are too lucrative. When your incentives delay overall goal achievement by more than one month, they need to be reduced. You may also want to consider limiting access to your money.

It is very likely that either you or your spouse will need barriers setup to ensure the household budget plan is properly followed. One or both of you probably can't handle convenient access to the checking and savings accounts, and need to limit this access. There are several ways you can make accessing your money more difficult. Most banks offer savings accounts and certificate of deposit accounts that come with penalties for early or too frequent withdrawals. You could also look into using online banks that don't have many local ATM machines. If those methods don't work, try having a trustworthy money manager keep this money in an account for you, but be careful. You don't want to give someone your money without doing your research. Make sure this money manager has a great reputation, offers insurance, and is very visible to the public. The last thing you need is someone stealing money from you.

9

DIVORCE

The second worst possible outcome of an ongoing marital dispute is divorce; because any level of physical abuse is worse. It causes a family to separate, and a lifetime bond to be broken. Children often lose some level of emotional security because of it. A support system is lost. Both husbands and wives become more likely to endure another failed relationship when it occurs. These emotional trials created by divorce are just plain ugly, but once financial impacts are added to them, they can seem unbearable.

The first major divorce related expense is typically related to hiring an attorney. They are often hired when couples can't agree on separation terms. When this happens the household must be split up, and the custody of children becomes a debate. Ownership of property has to be negotiated. Loans which were co-signed need to be addressed. Everything that was built for the household is now to be broken apart, and it all comes at a price. How much of a price depends on the couple and economy, but none of it is free.

Today, the average cost of a divorce in the U.S. is $15,000, and the median household income is around $51,000. Based on these numbers, the average U.S.

household has to give up nearly one third of its net worth to separate, and that's before any money or rights are awarded. Many of these costs can be tied to the long negotiation process most couples partake in before a final settlement has been reached or created by an arbitrator or judge. Unfortunately, it is rarely easy for divorcing couples to come to an agreement, but that's to be expected. These are the same people that couldn't survive their marriage. How can we expect them to agree on financial matters while dissolving their marriage? It's just not realistic, unless there was a prenuptial agreement. As a result, this process becomes more expensive, and attorneys love it. Even when a settlement has been arranged, the process may not be complete. Each state has its own divorce laws and appeals processes. If an appeal is accepted, more years can be added to a divorce case, and the costs will keep rising. But let's just say that a divorcing couple has their marital disputes decided by a judge, that doesn't necessarily end the headache and financial issues. While courts can decided who gets what after the marriage is officially over, these rulings mean little to financial institutions.

Banks do not care who is ruled responsible for debts owed to them in divorce cases. Whoever originally agreed to pay back the debt is ultimately responsible for the debt, even when another party has been ruled responsible. No judge can force a financial institution to remove the name of the person who was ruled not responsible for the debt from an account. They can't force the bank to stop reporting the debt under the non-responsible party's name. A contract was signed when the debt was created, and the court's rulings do not supersede that agreement, unless it is proven to be fraudulent. For those with the funds, a possible way out of this headache is to pay the debt and have the judge order their former spouse to reimburse the money. What does all of this mean for those unable to pay the debt themselves? Negative credit marks and lower credit scores will remain despite a court ruling. It also leads to higher rates on loans, and could even impact job eligibility. Divorce rulings are public records, and will show up during most employer background checks. And while a divorce should not impact an employer's decision-making process while screening for potential workers, people do use this as an excuse not to hire someone. Let's face it; proving that someone is discriminating based on marital status or divorce rulings is impossible because it is not recognized as such from a legal standpoint. These are just a few of the financial impacts divorce can have on couples. It gets even more expensive and ugly when children are involved.

Children suffer the most when their parents' divorce. They no longer have a home with their mother and father. A piece of their security is taken away, and is rarely ever replaced. They become emotional hostages to the problems of their parents despite their lack of contributions to any marital problems. But, when it comes to financial matters, the parents will likely suffer the most. Some divorcées are forced to separate from their children and provide more money for their care than what was spent before the household separated. Others will have to take on the full financial responsibility of raising their children because their ex-spouse refuses to help. Both scenarios can be financially devastating for either parent, but everyone loses in the second example. The children are not receiving the financial care they need. One parent has to take on all the expenses of raising a child alone. The other parent refuses to be a productive member of society by avoiding work or attempting to flee imprisonment. Another adult may have to depend on government assistance to provide for this newly single parent household. It's simply a devastating situation, but there are still other financial fallouts from divorce.

Though losing financial assets isn't as painful as losing children or support for the children, it is still unpleasant; especially when it comes in the form of spousal support. Image having to provide support for someone you no longer love for the rest of his or her life. Talk about being bitter. That's like having to literally pay for one mistake for the rest of your life. It's just an uncomfortable situation, and don't be fooled into thinking this only happens to celebrities. Regular people are hit with a spousal support awards, better known as alimony, too. When alimony is awarded, the payment structure is heavily determined by the courts and the laws of the state in which the divorce is filled. If you live in a state where the lower wage earner is regularly awarded with alimony despite wages earned, the chances of not having to part with all or most personal assets are very slim. Some of those states are Arizona, California, Idaho, Louisiana, Nevada, New Mexico, Texas, Washington, and Wisconsin due to their community property laws. In most other states, equal distribution laws are followed, which means property acquired during the marriage belongs to the spouse who earned it.

The other side of alimony isn't as pretty as it's portrayed either. Though there may be some initial joy in being rewarded with alimony, it becomes less glamorous over time. The house, car, jewelry, and even monetary support being received don't come without a constant reminder of a failed marriage. The car he or she bought you as a Christmas gift. The house you designed together, and raised your children in. Even the money awarded after the divorce is final can be a reminder of the inability to fully support oneself. Both sides of alimony come with drawbacks.

When households separate all financial progression is lost. It doesn't matter who brings what to the table, everyone take a few steps backwards. Two people were working together or separately to grow the net-worth of one household and that progression is halted. For some couples, this means decades of working towards building a combined estate was done for nothing, from a financial perspective. Others with only a few years under their belt and no children aren't impacted as much, but still have to start over again. Imagine living in a four bedroom, single family home and then having to move into a one bedroom apartment to rebuild your finances. While this may not be a big deal when you're in your mid-twenties, it can be much more depressing when you are over the age of thirty. Most adults begin to build their savings and increase net -worth in their thirties. Having to restart delays this process for several years and often prolongs retirement. Even divorcees that leave the marriage with enough funds to sustain the lifestyle they enjoyed while married will suffer some setbacks. They may have been on pace to retire earlier or build their estate faster had the marriage continued, but this is a best case scenario. Financially speaking, the worst outcome from a divorce would be losing all ability to build personal net -worth, and it happens more often than most realize. I've seen it firsthand.

One of my close family members is living this reality. He was married for about ten years and had four children, but is now divorced. Once he and his wife split up, he lost custody of his children, and had to leave the house that was in her name. This meant he had to start over from scratch. While he was living with his wife and family, he could afford to pay for school and was very close to becoming a registered nurse, but couldn't keep up the pace after the divorce. Not only did this slow down his career growth, but he also couldn't save any of his income. The amount of money he had to pay for child support and alimony left him with close to nothing for himself. Now, I'm not saying he shouldn't have had to pay these expenses because he was responsible for the welfare of his children. I'm just pointing out the fact that doing so caused him financial hardships. Today, he is over the age of fifty and still hasn't been able to build a lifestyle equivalent to the one he had when he was married. There is no telling how long he will need to work before being able to retire comfortably, but it sure won't be by the age of sixty-five. Sadly, he is not the only person I know to be in this type of situation; there are many others out there dealing with the same reality. Could he and others like him have avoided these circumstances? Yes, but only if at least one of two events occurred. They either would have needed a prenuptial agreement or have stayed married until their children were old enough to take care of themselves.

A prenuptial agreement is a signed contract, which states the terms of the marriage and divorce, in the event that the marriage fails. They can include any stipulations a person wants such as weight requirements , adultery clauses, financial splits based on years married, travel restrictions, sex frequency requirements, swinging approvals, plastic surgery requirements , and so much more. Most people don't use these contracts, because they don't have much to lose, and those stipulations are hardly ever legally enforceable. Between ages twenty-four and twenty-eight, which is when most Americans get married, people usually haven't accumulated many assets or wealth. Therefore, it is easy to understand why most young adults don't care to sign a prenuptial agreement. The large majority of those that do sign a prenuptial agreement are adults over thirty and adults who earn at least six figures per year. They are typically more established and have much more to lose. Personally, I'm not a big fan of them, but am not opposed either. I don't believe in walking into marriage with an escape plan, and am willing to risk losing my financial security. If that makes me vulnerable, so be it, but I can understand why someone would want to have this insurance. The only other way to be protected from the financial ramifications of divorce is to stay married.

It is never easy to put aside anger, resentment, distrust, and selfishness to preserve a marriage, but anyone that plans on being married until death must to take on this challenge. To do this, the divorce option has to be removed from the psyche. This doesn't mean that if there's physical abuse or adultery, the option to leave should be dismissed. Those are extreme circumstances. It's making a decision to stay despite the personal differences within the marriage. It's also finding reasons to remain optimistic when faced with circumstances that cause pessimist thoughts, especially when you're dealing with financial problems. Hopefully you thought about these things before getting married. The vows you took embodied these principles. Your vows and these principles go hand-in- hand, and if you didn't take your vows seriously, there is still time to adapt to them. Anyone can reach this level of commitment to staying married, but some people are not emotional fit for such a journey. The last thing anyone wants to see is a person slowly dying of depression just to stay in a marriage. If you plan on taking this mindset to preserve your marriage, make sure you consult a mental health professional first. There are no guarantees that your efforts will be rewarded, and you need to be prepared to deal with this reality. In addition to consulting a medical professional, I would recommend seeking spiritual counsel too. Take some time out of your day and really think about if you're ready to move forward with this level of commitment. You've already read about the financial ramifications of divorce, and have the information needed to make a financial decision. If you decide to leave the marriage, know that from a financial perspective, you are choosing to start over. However, if you choose to stay, know that you can only control yourself and will remain vulnerable. That is what marriage is all about anyway: the ability to be totally vulnerable to the actions of another human being. This is where the most beautiful and harmful part of marriage resides. You have to be willing to risk enduring harm, to reach the ultimate prize: agape love.

12 Month Budgeting Sheets

JANUARY BUDGET

MONTHLY INCOME
MONTHLY INCOME AFTER TAXES_____
MONTHLY INVESTMENT INCOME_____
MONTHLY INTEREST INCOME_____
TOTAL NET MONTHLY INCOME

MONTHLY LOAN EXPENSES
MORTGAGES_____
TUITION_____
AUTO LOANS_____
FEES_____
SCHOOL LOANS_____
SUPPLIES_____
PERSONAL LOANS_____
BOOKS_____
CREDIT CARDS_____
OTHER_____
TOTAL _____

SERVICE EXPENSES
GAS & ELECTRIC_____
 HAIR/SKIN CARE_____
WATER_____
DAYCARE_____
TRASH PICKUP_____
BABYSITTING_____
SEWAGE REMOVAL_____
INTERNET _____
GYM MEMBERSHIP_____
SECURITY_____
FITNESS INSTRUCTION_____
DRY CLEANING_____
ATHLETIC INSTRUCTION_____
CABLE/SATELITE_____
MUSIC LESSONS_____
HOME CLEANING_____
ACTING LESSONS_____
CELL/TELEPHONE_____
CHILD RELATED LESSONS_____
AUTO MAINTINANCE_____
MAGAZINE/NEWSPAPER_____
OTHER_____
TOTAL _____

MEDICAL EXPENSES

DENTAL_____

VISION_____

MEDICAL_____

INSURANCE_____

THERAPUDIC_____

OTHER_____

TOTAL _____

TRANSPORTATION EXPENSES

COSMETIC_____

GAS_____

PUBLIC TRANS_____

 RENTAL_____

TOLLS _____

OTHER_____

TOTAL _____

FOOD/HOME EXPENSES   **CLOTHING/LEISURE**
EXPENSES

GROCERIES_____

HOME INSURANCE_____

FARMING_____

FAST FOOD_____

TOTAL _____

CLOTHING/LEISURE EXPENSES

CLOTHES SHOPPING_____

OTHER SHOPPING _____

DATING_____

VACATIONS_____

OTHER_____

TOTAL_____

TOTAL ALL EXPENSES_____

TOTAL ALL INCOME_____

FEBURARY BUDGET
MONTHLY INCOME
MONTHLY INCOME AFTER TAXES_____
MONTHLY INVESTMENT INCOME_____
MONTHLY INTEREST INCOME_____
TOTAL NET MONTHLY INCOME_____

MONTHLY LOAN EXPENSES
MORTGAGES_____
TUITION_____
AUTO LOANS_____
FEES_____
SCHOOL LOANS_____
SUPPLIES_____
PERSONAL LOANS_____
BOOKS_____
CREDIT CARDS_____
OTHER_____
TOTAL _____

SERVICE EXPENSES
GAS & ELECTRIC_____
 HAIR/SKIN CARE_____
WATER_____
DAYCARE_____
TRASH PICKUP_____
BABYSITTING_____
SEWAGE REMOVAL_____
INTERNET _____
GYM MEMBERSHIP_____
SECURITY_____
FITNESS INSTRUCTION_____
DRY CLEANING_____
ATHLETIC INSTRUCTION_____
CABLE/SATELITE_____
MUSIC LESSONS_____
HOME CLEANING_____
ACTING LESSONS_____
CELL/TELEPHONE_____
CHILD RELATED LESSONS_____
AUTO MAINTINANCE_____
MAGAZINE/NEWSPAPER_____
OTHER_____
TOTAL _____

MEDICAL EXPENSES

DENTAL_____

VISION_____

MEDICAL_____

INSURANCE_____

THERAPUDIC_____

OTHER_____

TOTAL _____

TRANSPORTATION EXPENSES

COSMETIC_____

GAS_____

PUBLIC TRANS_____

 RENTAL_____

TOLLS _____

OTHER_____

TOTAL _____

FOOD/HOME EXPENSES   CLOTHING/LEISURE
EXPENSES

GROCERIES_____

HOME INSURANCE_____

FARMING_____

FAST FOOD_____

TOTAL _____

CLOTHING/LEISURE EXPENSES

CLOTHES SHOPPING_____

OTHER SHOPPING _____

DATING_____

VACATIONS_____

OTHER_____

TOTAL_____

TOTAL ALL EXPENSES_____

TOTAL ALL INCOME_____

MONTHLY INCOME

MONTHLY INCOME AFTER TAXES_____

MONTHLY INVESTMENT INCOME_____

MONTHLY INTEREST INCOME_____

TOTAL NET MONTHLY INCOME_____

MONTHLY LOAN EXPENSES

MORTGAGES_____

TUITION_____

AUTO LOANS_____

FEES_____

SCHOOL LOANS_____

SUPPLIES_____

PERSONAL LOANS_____

BOOKS_____

CREDIT CARDS_____

OTHER_____

TOTAL _____

SERVICE EXPENSES

GAS & ELECTRIC_____

HAIR/SKIN CARE_____

WATER_____

DAYCARE_____

TRASH PICKUP_____

BABYSITTING_____

SEWAGE REMOVAL_____

INTERNET _____

GYM MEMBERSHIP_____

SECURITY_____

FITNESS INSTRUCTION_____

DRY CLEANING_____

ATHLETIC INSTRUCTION_____

CABLE/SATELITE_____

MUSIC LESSONS_____

HOME CLEANING_____

ACTING LESSONS_____

CELL/TELEPHONE_____

CHILD RELATED LESSONS_____

AUTO MAINTINANCE_____

MAGAZINE/NEWSPAPER_____

OTHER_____

TOTAL _____

MEDICAL EXPENSES

DENTAL_____

VISION_____

MEDICAL_____

INSURANCE_____

THERAPUDIC_____

OTHER_____

TOTAL _____

TRANSPORTATION EXPENSES

COSMETIC_____

GAS_____

PUBLIC TRANS_____

 RENTAL_____

TOLLS _____

OTHER_____

TOTAL _____

FOOD/HOME EXPENSES   CLOTHING/LEISURE

EXPENSES

GROCERIES_____

HOME INSURANCE_____

FARMING_____

FAST FOOD_____

TOTAL _____

CLOTHING/LEISURE EXPENSES

CLOTHES SHOPPING_____

OTHER SHOPPING _____

DATING_____

VACATIONS_____

OTHER_____

TOTAL_____

TOTAL ALL EXPENSES_____

TOTAL ALL INCOME_____

MONTHLY INCOME
MONTHLY INCOME AFTER TAXES_____
MONTHLY INVESTMENT INCOME_____
MONTHLY INTEREST INCOME_____
TOTAL NET MONTHLY INCOME_____

MONTHLY LOAN EXPENSES
MORTGAGES_____
TUITION_____
AUTO LOANS_____
FEES_____
SCHOOL LOANS_____
SUPPLIES_____
PERSONAL LOANS_____
BOOKS_____
CREDIT CARDS_____
OTHER_____
TOTAL _____

SERVICE EXPENSES
GAS & ELECTRIC_____
 HAIR/SKIN CARE_____
WATER_____
DAYCARE_____
TRASH PICKUP_____
BABYSITTING_____
SEWAGE REMOVAL_____
INTERNET _____
GYM MEMBERSHIP_____
SECURITY_____
FITNESS INSTRUCTION_____
DRY CLEANING_____
ATHLETIC INSTRUCTION_____
CABLE/SATELITE_____
MUSIC LESSONS_____
HOME CLEANING_____
ACTING LESSONS_____
CELL/TELEPHONE_____
CHILD RELATED LESSONS_____
AUTO MAINTINANCE_____
MAGAZINE/NEWSPAPER_____
OTHER_____
TOTAL _____

MEDICAL EXPENSES
DENTAL_____
VISION_____
MEDICAL_____
INSURANCE_____
THERAPUDIC_____
OTHER_____
TOTAL

TRANSPORTATION EXPENSES
COSMETIC_____
GAS_____
PUBLIC TRANS_____
 RENTAL_____
TOLLS _____
OTHER_____
TOTAL

FOOD/HOME EXPENSES   **CLOTHING/LEISURE**
EXPENSES
GROCERIES_____
HOME INSURANCE_____
FARMING_____
FAST FOOD_____
TOTAL

CLOTHING/LEISURE EXPENSES
CLOTHES SHOPPING_____
OTHER SHOPPING _____
DATING_____
VACATIONS_____
OTHER_____
TOTAL

TOTAL ALL EXPENSES____
TOTAL ALL INCOME_____

MAY BUDGET

MONTHLY INCOME
MONTHLY INCOME AFTER TAXES_____
MONTHLY INVESTMENT INCOME_____
MONTHLY INTEREST INCOME_____
TOTAL NET MONTHLY INCOME_____

MONTHLY LOAN EXPENSES
MORTGAGES_____
TUITION_____
AUTO LOANS_____
FEES_____
SCHOOL LOANS_____
SUPPLIES_____
PERSONAL LOANS_____
BOOKS_____
CREDIT CARDS_____
OTHER_____
TOTAL _____

SERVICE EXPENSES
GAS & ELECTRIC_____
HAIR/SKIN CARE_____
WATER_____
DAYCARE_____
TRASH PICKUP_____
BABYSITTING_____
SEWAGE REMOVAL_____
INTERNET _____
GYM MEMBERSHIP_____
SECURITY_____
FITNESS INSTRUCTION_____
DRY CLEANING_____
ATHLETIC INSTRUCTION_____
CABLE/SATELITE_____
MUSIC LESSONS_____
HOME CLEANING_____
ACTING LESSONS_____
CELL/TELEPHONE_____
CHILD RELATED LESSONS_____
AUTO MAINTINANCE_____
MAGAZINE/NEWSPAPER_____
OTHER_____
TOTAL _____

MEDICAL EXPENSES
DENTAL_____
VISION_____
MEDICAL_____
INSURANCE_____
THERAPUDIC_____
OTHER_____
TOTAL _____

TRANSPORTATION EXPENSES
COSMETIC_____
GAS_____
PUBLIC TRANS_____
 RENTAL_____
TOLLS _____
OTHER_____
TOTAL _____

FOOD/HOME EXPENSES   CLOTHING/LEISURE
EXPENSES
GROCERIES_____
HOME INSURANCE_____
FARMING_____
FAST FOOD_____
TOTAL _____

CLOTHING/LEISURE EXPENSES
CLOTHES SHOPPING_____
OTHER SHOPPING _____
DATING_____
VACATIONS_____
OTHER_____
TOTAL_____

TOTAL ALL EXPENSES_____
TOTAL ALL INCOME_____

MONTHLY INCOME

MONTHLY INCOME AFTER TAXES_____

MONTHLY INVESTMENT INCOME_____

MONTHLY INTEREST INCOME_____

TOTAL NET MONTHLY INCOME_____

MONTHLY LOAN EXPENSES

MORTGAGES_____

TUITION_____

AUTO LOANS_____

FEES_____

SCHOOL LOANS_____

SUPPLIES_____

PERSONAL LOANS_____

BOOKS_____

CREDIT CARDS_____

OTHER_____

TOTAL _____

SERVICE EXPENSES

GAS & ELECTRIC_____

HAIR/SKIN CARE_____

WATER_____

DAYCARE_____

TRASH PICKUP_____

BABYSITTING_____

SEWAGE REMOVAL_____

INTERNET _____

GYM MEMBERSHIP_____

SECURITY_____

FITNESS INSTRUCTION_____

DRY CLEANING_____

ATHLETIC INSTRUCTION_____

CABLE/SATELITE_____

MUSIC LESSONS_____

HOME CLEANING_____

ACTING LESSONS_____

CELL/TELEPHONE_____

CHILD RELATED LESSONS_____

AUTO MAINTINANCE_____

MAGAZINE/NEWSPAPER_____

OTHER_____

TOTAL _____

MEDICAL EXPENSES
DENTAL_____
VISION_____
MEDICAL_____
INSURANCE_____
THERAPUDIC_____
OTHER_____
TOTAL _____

TRANSPORTATION EXPENSES
COSMETIC_____
GAS_____
PUBLIC TRANS_____
 RENTAL_____
TOLLS _____
OTHER_____
TOTAL _____

FOOD/HOME EXPENSES   CLOTHING/LEISURE
EXPENSES
GROCERIES_____
HOME INSURANCE_____
FARMING_____
FAST FOOD_____
TOTAL _____

CLOTHING/LEISURE EXPENSES
CLOTHES SHOPPING_____
OTHER SHOPPING _____
DATING_____
VACATIONS_____
OTHER_____
TOTAL_____

TOTAL ALL EXPENSES_____
TOTAL ALL INCOME_____

JULY BUDGET

MONTHLY INCOME
MONTHLY INCOME AFTER TAXES_____
MONTHLY INVESTMENT INCOME_____
MONTHLY INTEREST INCOME_____
TOTAL NET MONTHLY INCOME_____

MONTHLY LOAN EXPENSES
MORTGAGES_____
TUITION_____
AUTO LOANS_____
FEES_____
SCHOOL LOANS_____
SUPPLIES_____
PERSONAL LOANS_____
BOOKS_____
CREDIT CARDS_____
OTHER_____
TOTAL _____

SERVICE EXPENSES
GAS & ELECTRIC_____
 HAIR/SKIN CARE_____
WATER_____
DAYCARE_____
TRASH PICKUP_____
BABYSITTING_____
SEWAGE REMOVAL_____
INTERNET _____
GYM MEMBERSHIP_____
SECURITY_____
FITNESS INSTRUCTION_____
DRY CLEANING_____
ATHLETIC INSTRUCTION_____
CABLE/SATELITE_____
MUSIC LESSONS_____
HOME CLEANING_____
ACTING LESSONS_____
CELL/TELEPHONE_____
CHILD RELATED LESSONS_____
AUTO MAINTINANCE_____
MAGAZINE/NEWSPAPER_____
OTHER_____
TOTAL _____

MEDICAL EXPENSES

DENTAL_____

VISION_____

MEDICAL_____

INSURANCE_____

THERAPUDIC_____

OTHER_____

TOTAL _____

TRANSPORTATION EXPENSES

COSMETIC_____

GAS_____

PUBLIC TRANS_____

 RENTAL_____

TOLLS _____

OTHER_____

TOTAL _____

FOOD/HOME EXPENSES   CLOTHING/LEISURE
EXPENSES

GROCERIES_____

HOME INSURANCE_____

FARMING_____

FAST FOOD_____

TOTAL _____

CLOTHING/LEISURE EXPENSES

CLOTHES SHOPPING_____

OTHER SHOPPING _____

DATING_____

VACATIONS_____

OTHER_____

TOTAL_____

TOTAL ALL EXPENSES_____

TOTAL ALL INCOME_____

MONTHLY INCOME
MONTHLY INCOME AFTER TAXES_____
MONTHLY INVESTMENT INCOME_____
MONTHLY INTEREST INCOME_____
TOTAL NET MONTHLY INCOME_____

MONTHLY LOAN EXPENSES
MORTGAGES_____
TUITION_____
AUTO LOANS_____
FEES_____
SCHOOL LOANS_____
SUPPLIES_____
PERSONAL LOANS_____
BOOKS_____
CREDIT CARDS_____
OTHER_____
TOTAL _____

SERVICE EXPENSES
GAS & ELECTRIC_____
 HAIR/SKIN CARE_____
WATER_____
DAYCARE_____
TRASH PICKUP_____
BABYSITTING_____
SEWAGE REMOVAL_____
INTERNET _____
GYM MEMBERSHIP_____
SECURITY_____
FITNESS INSTRUCTION_____
DRY CLEANING_____
ATHLETIC INSTRUCTION_____
CABLE/SATELITE_____
MUSIC LESSONS_____
HOME CLEANING_____
ACTING LESSONS_____
CELL/TELEPHONE_____
CHILD RELATED LESSONS_____
AUTO MAINTINANCE_____
MAGAZINE/NEWSPAPER_____
OTHER_____
TOTAL _____

MEDICAL EXPENSES

DENTAL_____

VISION_____

MEDICAL_____

INSURANCE_____

THERAPUDIC_____

OTHER_____

TOTAL _____

TRANSPORTATION EXPENSES

COSMETIC_____

GAS_____

PUBLIC TRANS_____

 RENTAL_____

TOLLS _____

OTHER_____

TOTAL _____

FOOD/HOME EXPENSES   **CLOTHING/LEISURE**
EXPENSES

GROCERIES_____

HOME INSURANCE_____

FARMING_____

FAST FOOD_____

TOTAL _____

CLOTHING/LEISURE EXPENSES

CLOTHES SHOPPING_____

OTHER SHOPPING _____

DATING_____

VACATIONS_____

OTHER_____

TOTAL_____

TOTAL ALL EXPENSES_____

TOTAL ALL INCOME_____

SEPTEMBER BUDGET

MONTHLY INCOME
MONTHLY INCOME AFTER TAXES_____
MONTHLY INVESTMENT INCOME_____
MONTHLY INTEREST INCOME_____
TOTAL NET MONTHLY INCOME_____

MONTHLY LOAN EXPENSES
MORTGAGES_____
TUITION_____
AUTO LOANS_____
FEES_____
SCHOOL LOANS_____
SUPPLIES_____
PERSONAL LOANS_____
BOOKS_____
CREDIT CARDS_____
OTHER_____
TOTAL _____

SERVICE EXPENSES
GAS & ELECTRIC_____
 HAIR/SKIN CARE_____
WATER_____
DAYCARE_____
TRASH PICKUP_____
BABYSITTING_____
SEWAGE REMOVAL_____
INTERNET _____
GYM MEMBERSHIP_____
SECURITY_____
FITNESS INSTRUCTION_____
DRY CLEANING_____
ATHLETIC INSTRUCTION_____
CABLE/SATELITE_____
MUSIC LESSONS_____
HOME CLEANING_____
ACTING LESSONS_____
CELL/TELEPHONE_____
CHILD RELATED LESSONS_____
AUTO MAINTINANCE_____
MAGAZINE/NEWSPAPER_____
OTHER_____
TOTAL _____

MEDICAL EXPENSES
DENTAL_____
VISION_____
MEDICAL_____
INSURANCE_____
THERAPUDIC_____
OTHER_____
TOTAL _____

TRANSPORTATION EXPENSES
COSMETIC_____
GAS_____
PUBLIC TRANS_____
 RENTAL_____
TOLLS _____
OTHER_____
TOTAL _____

FOOD/HOME EXPENSES   **CLOTHING/LEISURE**
EXPENSES
GROCERIES_____
HOME INSURANCE_____
FARMING_____
FAST FOOD_____
TOTAL _____

CLOTHING/LEISURE EXPENSES
CLOTHES SHOPPING_____
OTHER SHOPPING _____
DATING_____
VACATIONS_____
OTHER_____
TOTAL_____

TOTAL ALL EXPENSES_____
TOTAL ALL INCOME_____

OCTOBER BUDGET

MONTHLY INCOME
MONTHLY INCOME AFTER TAXES_____
MONTHLY INVESTMENT INCOME_____
MONTHLY INTEREST INCOME_____
TOTAL NET MONTHLY INCOME_____

MONTHLY LOAN EXPENSES
MORTGAGES_____
TUITION_____
AUTO LOANS_____
FEES_____
SCHOOL LOANS_____
SUPPLIES_____
PERSONAL LOANS_____
BOOKS_____
CREDIT CARDS_____
OTHER_____
TOTAL _____

SERVICE EXPENSES
GAS & ELECTRIC_____
 HAIR/SKIN CARE_____
WATER_____
DAYCARE_____
TRASH PICKUP_____
BABYSITTING_____
SEWAGE REMOVAL_____
INTERNET _____
GYM MEMBERSHIP_____
SECURITY_____
FITNESS INSTRUCTION_____
DRY CLEANING_____
ATHLETIC INSTRUCTION_____
CABLE/SATELITE_____
MUSIC LESSONS_____
HOME CLEANING_____
ACTING LESSONS_____
CELL/TELEPHONE_____
CHILD RELATED LESSONS_____
AUTO MAINTINANCE_____
MAGAZINE/NEWSPAPER_____
OTHER_____
TOTAL _____

MEDICAL EXPENSES

DENTAL_____

VISION_____

MEDICAL_____

INSURANCE_____

THERAPUDIC_____

OTHER_____

TOTAL _____

TRANSPORTATION EXPENSES

COSMETIC_____

GAS_____

PUBLIC TRANS_____

RENTAL_____

TOLLS _____

OTHER_____

TOTAL _____

FOOD/HOME EXPENSES   CLOTHING/LEISURE
EXPENSES

GROCERIES_____

HOME INSURANCE_____

FARMING_____

FAST FOOD_____

TOTAL _____

CLOTHING/LEISURE EXPENSES

CLOTHES SHOPPING_____

OTHER SHOPPING _____

DATING_____

VACATIONS_____

OTHER_____

TOTAL_____

TOTAL ALL EXPENSES_____

TOTAL ALL INCOME_____

MONTHLY INCOME

MONTHLY INCOME AFTER TAXES_____

MONTHLY INVESTMENT INCOME_____

MONTHLY INTEREST INCOME_____

TOTAL NET MONTHLY INCOME_____

MONTHLY LOAN EXPENSES

MORTGAGES_____

TUITION_____

AUTO LOANS_____

FEES_____

SCHOOL LOANS_____

SUPPLIES_____

PERSONAL LOANS_____

BOOKS_____

CREDIT CARDS_____

OTHER_____

TOTAL _____

SERVICE EXPENSES

GAS & ELECTRIC_____

 HAIR/SKIN CARE_____

WATER_____

DAYCARE_____

TRASH PICKUP_____

BABYSITTING_____

SEWAGE REMOVAL_____

INTERNET _____

GYM MEMBERSHIP_____

SECURITY_____

FITNESS INSTRUCTION_____

DRY CLEANING_____

ATHLETIC INSTRUCTION_____

CABLE/SATELITE_____

MUSIC LESSONS_____

HOME CLEANING_____

ACTING LESSONS_____

CELL/TELEPHONE_____

CHILD RELATED LESSONS_____

AUTO MAINTINANCE_____

MAGAZINE/NEWSPAPER_____

OTHER_____

TOTAL _____

MEDICAL EXPENSES
DENTAL_____
VISION_____
MEDICAL_____
INSURANCE_____
THERAPUDIC_____
OTHER_____
TOTAL _____

TRANSPORTATION EXPENSES
COSMETIC_____
GAS_____
PUBLIC TRANS_____
 RENTAL_____
TOLLS _____
OTHER_____
TOTAL _____

FOOD/HOME EXPENSES   **CLOTHING/LEISURE**
EXPENSES
GROCERIES_____
HOME INSURANCE_____
FARMING_____
FAST FOOD_____
TOTAL _____

CLOTHING/LEISURE EXPENSES
CLOTHES SHOPPING_____
OTHER SHOPPING _____
DATING_____
VACATIONS_____
OTHER_____
TOTAL_____

TOTAL ALL EXPENSES_____
TOTAL ALL INCOME_____

DECEMBER BUDGET

MONTHLY INCOME
MONTHLY INCOME AFTER TAXES_____
MONTHLY INVESTMENT INCOME_____
MONTHLY INTEREST INCOME_____
TOTAL NET MONTHLY INCOME_____

MONTHLY LOAN EXPENSES
MORTGAGES_____
TUITION_____
AUTO LOANS_____
FEES_____
SCHOOL LOANS_____
SUPPLIES_____
PERSONAL LOANS_____
BOOKS_____
CREDIT CARDS_____
OTHER_____
TOTAL _____

SERVICE EXPENSES
GAS & ELECTRIC_____
 HAIR/SKIN CARE_____
WATER_____
DAYCARE_____
TRASH PICKUP_____
BABYSITTING_____
SEWAGE REMOVAL_____
INTERNET _____
GYM MEMBERSHIP_____
SECURITY_____
FITNESS INSTRUCTION_____
DRY CLEANING_____
ATHLETIC INSTRUCTION_____
CABLE/SATELITE_____
MUSIC LESSONS_____
HOME CLEANING_____
ACTING LESSONS_____
CELL/TELEPHONE_____
CHILD RELATED LESSONS_____
AUTO MAINTINANCE_____
MAGAZINE/NEWSPAPER_____
OTHER_____
TOTAL _____

MEDICAL EXPENSES
DENTAL_____
VISION_____
MEDICAL_____
INSURANCE_____
THERAPUDIC_____
OTHER_____
TOTAL _____

TRANSPORTATION EXPENSES
COSMETIC_____
GAS_____
PUBLIC TRANS_____
 RENTAL_____
TOLLS _____
OTHER_____
TOTAL _____

FOOD/HOME EXPENSES   CLOTHING/LEISURE
EXPENSES
GROCERIES_____
HOME INSURANCE_____
FARMING_____
FAST FOOD_____
TOTAL _____

CLOTHING/LEISURE EXPENSES
CLOTHES SHOPPING_____
OTHER SHOPPING _____
DATING_____
VACATIONS_____
OTHER_____
TOTAL_____

TOTAL ALL EXPENSES_____
TOTAL ALL INCOME_____

About the Author

Joseph Lorick was born August 25th 1981 in Baltimore, MD. He graduated from the 3rd oldest active high school in the country, Baltimore City College, in 1999. He then went on to earn his bachelors in business administration from Bowie State University. As a senior, Joseph began his career in banking and has never stopped. He has over eleven years of experience as a debt management advisor, credit analyst, mortgage advisor, consumer loans analyst, and strategies analyst. During this time, Joseph has spoken with thousands of customers and gained extensive knowledge about the financial habits of American citizens. Joseph is also a Christian, and has been for the last twenty years. He works in the church as a financial counselor and also serves as a worship coordinator. During his spare time, he leads financial freedom lectures and assists his community by teaching financial literacy. He is a strong believer in social progression through education and writes to further this cause.

To receive daily debt tips and other helpful financial advice, follow Joseph Lorick on Facebook, Twitter (@DidEvthButThink, or Instagram @MrDEBT.

You can also visit
www.moneyetiquette.com
for great debt management tips!